& THE UNITED NATIONS

by Faye Carroll

UNIVERSITY OF KENTUCKY PRESS
LEXINGTON · 1967

DT
714
C3

1/15/69 Eastern 4.80

Squires

54813

L. P. 1/10/69

SOUTH WEST AFRICA
AND THE UNITED NATIONS

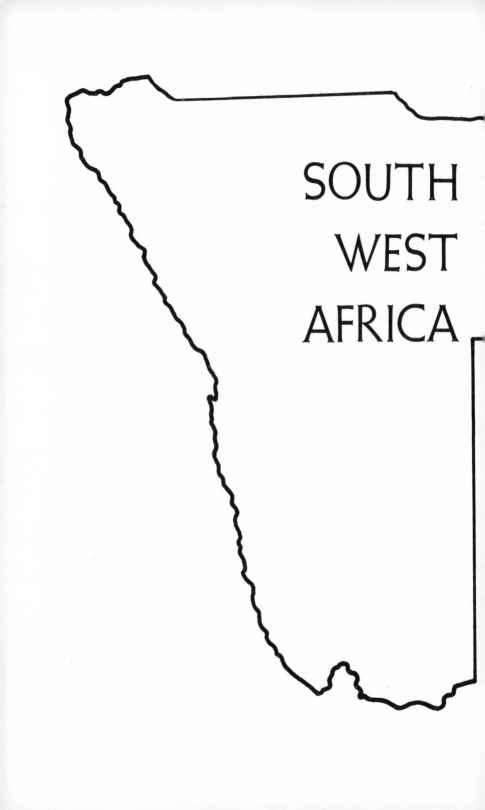

SOUTH

WEST

AFRICA

PREFACE

As the only League of Nations mandate which has been neither granted independence nor placed under the United Nations Trusteeship System, South West Africa is the focus of a long-standing dispute over jurisdiction between the Republic of South Africa and the United Nations. The Republic of South Africa has administered the mandate for forty-five years, but its right to control has been challenged several times within the United Nations. Most of these challenges have been based on two factors —the policy of *apartheid* (racial separation) which South Africa has applied to the area and the slow rate of progress in self-government, economics, and education within South West Africa. In actuality, the progressive development of the native population has been precluded by application of apartheid, the most despised and outdated racial policy in existence today.

More than a political, legal, and moral dispute between the South African government and the United Nations, the South West Africa case is a reflection of two revolutionary movements which have dominated world politics in recent years. These movements seek the eradication of the last vestiges of colonialism and racial discrimination.

The purpose of this study is to provide a historical background to the dispute, reviewing the actions of the United Nations and of the South African government, evaluating the effectiveness of the U.N. in this matter, and considering the probable future consequences of the dispute. Chapter one outlines in detail the policy of apartheid, essential to the explanation of the motivating force in this case. Important political and legal issues are involved, but unlike apartheid, these issues likely could be settled by negotiation. Chapter two explains the nature of South Africa's international mandate in which that government promised to promote to the utmost the material and moral well-being of the mandate's inhabitants and to submit its administration to supervision by the League of Nations. This mandate gave South Africa extensive powers over South West Africa, but, contrary to claims of some South African officials, South Africa was not granted sovereignty over the territory. Chapter three traces and compares criticisms by the League and by the United Nations of South Africa's native policy and its attempts to annex the mandate. Because of the different compositions of these two organizations and because the evolving changes in international attitudes toward colonialism and racism, the United Nations has been far more critical of South Africa than was the League. Chapter four deals with the legal bases of jurisdiction over the mandate. The United Nations has the legal authority to supervise the administration of South West Africa, but it does not possess the legal means to establish satisfactory supervision. Chapter five outlines the methods of supervision available to the United Nations and considers their limitations. The mandate concept of "a sacred trust of civilization" required cooperation between the mandatory power and the League of Nations; South Africa has been uncooperative, however, and the legal remedies available to the United Nations are limited. The U.N.'s many attempts to reach a compromise solution of the South West Africa issue are discussed in chapter six. Thus far, all attempts at compromise have failed, not because of a lack of effort or because of legal issues, but because of the policy of apartheid. Chapter seven considers efforts by the United Nations to establish itself as a dominant force in South West Africa. Thus far, the United Nations has used no sanctions, and it has failed to secure cooperation from South Africa. Chapter eight, in evaluating the United Nations' performance in the South West Africa case, demonstrates that while the organization has been successful in achieving a degree of supervision over the mandate and has kept the issue before world attention, it has failed to achieve its major objectives. Nevertheless, South African policy is so outdated by modern political standards that ultimately it is untenable. Whether or not the United Nations can be a guiding force for peaceful change in South West Africa is uncertain at this point.

Any study of the South West Africa issue is limited somewhat by the lack of objective data about conditions within the territory. The Republic government has been unreceptive to attempts by the United Nations to make an impartial survey of conditions within the mandates area. The scholar is forced to weigh statements made by South African officials against those made by travelers, refugees, and exiled leaders. This same limitation, it should be noted, impedes the work of the members of the United Nations and of the International Court of Justice.

In the preparation of this manuscript I am indebted to many people. The greatest expression of appreciation is due Dr. Amry Vandenbosch, who suggested the topic, and provided and translated a portion of the research materials.

I also wish to thank Dr. Herbert Drennon, Dr. James Hopkins, Dr. Enno Kraehe, Mr. Robert Rodes, and Dr. Max Wasserman for their constructive criticism and suggestions; and Dr. John M. Howell for his suggestions concerning the revision of this manuscript. Finally, to my parents, Mr. and Mrs. Wilburn Carroll, goes a well-earned expression of appreciation.

FAYE CARROLL

CONTENTS

ONE:

A POLITICAL ANACHRONISM

Africa in the twentieth century has undergone a rapid and extensive transformation which has expressed itself in national independence and self-determination for black Africans. One may debate the wisdom of independence and self-determination for some African states, but these are the dominant themes of this century, just as colonialism and white supremacy were the accepted values of an earlier era. For better or for worse, most native Africans wish to control their own countries. In some areas of Africa, however, the natives still are denied the most basic human rights. In particular, the political, economic, and social systems of South West Africa, along with those of neighboring South Africa, Angola, and Rhodesia, do not conform to twentieth-century standards. The established systems of rule in these areas were always unjust; they now are archaic.

Only against this background can one understand the modern dilemma in South West Africa. If most of the African states were still under colonial domination and if policies of white supremacy did not predominate in southern Africa, the South West Africa dispute would not exist. Only by analyzing existing conditions in South West Africa can one understand the significance of this comparatively unknown territory to the United Nations and to the South African government. In part, this significance stems from geographic and economic factors, but the primary one is South Africa's racial policy.

The relative lack of natural resources within South West Africa, especially in comparison with other African nations, has been partially responsible for its precarious political position. Had it been a wealthier region, South West Africa would have attracted world attention sooner than it did. A sparsely populated desert region with poorly developed communication and transportation facilities, South West Africa has little internal unity and is dependent upon South Africa for maintenance of its economic system. Geographically, the country's 317,725 square mile area[1] (making it about one-third larger than France or three-fourths the size of the Republic of South Africa)[2] is bounded by Portuguese Angola on the north, the Atlantic Ocean on the west, Cape Colony on the south, and Bechuanaland on the east. The interior plateau, almost mountainous in parts, has an average annual rainfall of fifteen inches. The southern portion, from the Orange River to approximately seventy miles south of the city of Windhoek, is hot and dry, but it does support some stock farming. The area north of Windhoek, which is located near the geographic center of the territory and is the administrative capital of South West Africa, is cooler in climate and is the section where most of the whites in the territory reside. Farming and karakul sheep raising are practiced in the central portion of the territory, and grazing lands are found in the northern portions.[3]

Desert areas and the swamp regions of the Okavango River discourage travel, but the territory has two major ports at Walvis Bay and Angra Pequena or Lüderitsbucht.

The population of South West Africa, small because of the dryness of the land, is racially heterogeneous with the colored or native population heavily outnumbering the white or European population.[4] The estimated total population in 1965 was 574,000 —75,000 white or European and 499,000 colored or native.[5] These figures represent a considerable increase in both the white and

[1] This is exclusive of Walvis Bay, an area of 374 square miles which forms an integral part of Cape Province, but which is administered with South West Africa as a matter of convenience.

[2] On October 6, 1960, the white population of South Africa voted in favor of the formation of a republic. Both the terms Union of South Africa and Republic of South Africa will be used in this study.

[3] *South West Africa and the Union of South Africa: The History of the Mandate* (New York: Union of South Africa Information Office, 1946), 24-26.

[4] The term "colored" refers to racial mixtures. For statistical purposes, this group is often classified with the natives. The terms "white" and "European" are used interchangeably.

[5] United Nations, General Assembly, *Journal* (1965), 123.

nonwhite populations since South Africa's administration of the territory began. Some members of the United Nations have accused the Republic of South Africa of following policies leading to the extermination of natives, but there is little evidence to substantiate this charge.

Additionally, the ethnic origins of the racial groups are extremely heterogeneous. The territory's European population is composed of Afrikaners, Germans, and English. The Afrikaners are Boers or South Africans of Dutch descent who outnumber the Germans and the English almost two to one. To simplify matters, the native population commonly is subdivided into six groups—the Bergdamara, the Bushmen, the Hottentots, the Herero, the Ovambo, and the Bastards. Some of these groups have advanced little beyond the tribal state.

For hundreds of years the basic social issue in South Africa was racial rivalry between the Dutch, the Germans, and the English. Now the basic conflict is between the Europeans and the non-Europeans. The situation in the Republic of South Africa and South West Africa differs somewhat from other territories in which there is a nonwhite majority, for in South Africa, a white nation has established itself on a black continent.[6]

The Europeans of the Republic of South Africa have advanced the policy of apartheid as the solution to the racial problems. The Republic government defines apartheid as the separate development of the white and native races. Outside the Republic, however, white supremacy is the most commonly used definition. Completely disregarding the spirit of international agreements, the Republic has been systematically and increasingly applying apartheid to the mandated territory of South West Africa.

In fairness to the whites of the Republic of South Africa and South West Africa, one must concede that with nonwhites outnumbering whites by nearly four to one and with the natives unskilled, uneducated, poverty-stricken, and culturally underdeveloped, a considerable problem arising from discrepant cultures

[6] Lawrence E. Neame, *The History of Apartheid* (London: Pall Mall Press, 1962), 9-20.

exists. Also, the white population fears the natives, not only because they are culturally different, but also because of their sheer numbers. Members of the Republic Parliament often voice the fear that if the natives were given economic and political power, they would use it to deprive whites of what they possess. The Republic's answer to this dilemma has been to deny the natives most educational, political, and economic opportunities.

Apartheid calls for the separate development of the races in segregated geographic areas, but this so far has been impossible economically. In 1913 the Parliament of the Union of South Africa passed the Natives Land Act, which set aside certain areas within the Union as native reserves. According to this act, it was illegal for a native to purchase land in a European area without the sanction of the governor-general. It also prohibited Europeans from acquiring land in native areas without an act of Parliament. The government had intended to segregate all natives on these reserves, but for all practical purposes, this plan of total segregation was abandoned because the demand for cheap native labor was too great. Many native laborers and domestic workers live within native settlements in the cities, and some farm laborers live on farms owned by Europeans. Recently, the South African government has reaffirmed its intention of restricting all natives to the reserves. However, this policy cannot be enforced without creating adverse effects on the economy of the Europeans, because the prosperity of the whites depends heavily upon cheap native labor.

Even if the economy of the Europeans could survive confinement of the natives to reserves, it is doubtful that the native economy could. Most of the reserves lack a sufficient supply of water; the land is poor; and agricultural production rarely rises above the subsistence level. Reserve land and produce are held in common by the residents, but many reserves produce no marketable goods, and natives are forced to find employment outside the reserves to pay taxes.[7]

[7] The Republic government refuses to estimate the amount of taxes a native must pay, but natives are subject to excise, import, and export fees as well as taxes on dogs and vehicles.

In 1920 the Union government allocated money to purchase native reserves in South West Africa. The natives were the original owners of the land, but most of their holdings had been confiscated by the German government, which annexed the territory in 1892 and sold or allotted these lands to Europeans. By 1903 only one-third of the colony was in the possession of the natives.[8] When Germany was defeated in World War I, the natives assumed that they would recover their lost land. The Union government concluded, however, that vested interests had resulted and that the lands could not be restored to the natives. Most of the German estates in the territory were not expropriated primarily because the South African government did not wish to alienate this white group.

In 1948, the South African government reported that 27,789,172 hectares (1 hectare equals 2.471 acres) of South West Africa's land were occupied by Europeans. Natives and colored residents occupied 17,361,589 and 1,303,400 hectares, respectively. An additional 1,260,000 hectares were classified as unoccupied lands.[9] The United Nations Trusteeship Council noted that the Europeans, who constituted less than 10 percent of the population, owned 58 percent of the territory.[10]

A system of police and unpoliced zones established in South West Africa restricts the travel limits of the natives and sometimes separates native families by limiting the right of a man who works in a police zone to visit freely with his family who lives in an unpoliced area. The entire territory is divided into police and unpoliced zones. The police zones comprises approximately five-eights of the territory, but it contains desert areas which are lightly populated. In essence, the police zone is the area of European settlement that has police protection and that is more directly under the governing influence of the Republic Parliament and

---

[8] Mary Ellen Townsend, *The Rise and Fall of Germany's Colonial Empire, 1884-1918* (New York: Macmillan Co., 1930), 283.
[9] United Nations, Trusteeship Council, *Official Records* (T/175, Dec., 1948), 81.
[10] *Trusteeship Records*, 3rd Sess. (July 23, 1948).

the Legislative Assembly of South West Africa. The unpoliced zone is an area of native settlement where, in theory, Republic rule is more indirect and the natives are accorded nominal tribal rule.

Almost all Europeans, as well as many natives, live inside the police zone. Natives may live in eighteen native reserves within this zone, or by special permission, they may live in a native location in an urban area or on a European farm where they work. In 1954 the minister of native affairs announced new regulations for native settlements in areas, requiring that new locations be built with a buffer zone of 500 yards between native residences and those of any other racial group.[11]

Natives within the police zone must obey strict travel and work regulations: no non-European within the police zone may buy a railway ticket, travel within, or leave the police zone without a pass issued for that purpose by his European employer or by officials specified by law; without a pass he may not go beyond the confines of the location, reserve, farm, or place where he resides or where he is employed; no nonresident of a particular location, reserve, or other area set aside for the occupation of natives may enter, reside in, or visit the area without a permit; no non-European may enter the police zone without a pass. The administrator also may declare that no native shall be in any public place within the area controlled by the local urban authority during specified hours of the night without a special permit.[12]

The South Africans maintain that the pass system does not discriminate, because Europeans must also have passes if they enter the unpoliced zone or the reserves. But the system of reserves, special location, and passes often results in inhumane treatment of the natives. A man who is working in an urban area may be denied a pass to visit his family in a reserve, or natives in one reserve may not be able to visit their families in other reserves.

---

[11] "Windhoek Crisis," *Africa Digest*, VII (Feb. 1960), 130-31.
[12] United Nations, Report of the Committee on South West Africa, 9th Sess., Supp. No. 14 (A/2666, 1954), 24.

If a native is dismissed from a job, or if his employer has not been satisfied with his work, he might not be granted a pass back to his reserve or to another job and then would be subject to arrest for traveling without a pass.

The disparity which exists between opportunities offered the European and the non-European populations can be discerned clearly by comparing their educational facilities. Only recently has any public education been offered to natives, and critics claim the education system perpetuates apartheid. One can say, as Republic defenders say, that the natives are not yet advanced to a stage where they can effectively use higher education, technical training, or political opportunities, such as voting, running for public office, and holding civil service jobs. This argument contains an element of truth, but after forty-five years of Republic administration this is no longer the primary consideration. The issue is whether or not the necessary steps toward native advancement have been taken.

The German government, which ruled South West Africa until World War I, provided no schools for the non-Europeans. The Germans left native education entirely to Catholic and Protestant missionary societies. Only 5,000 native children of approximately 65,000 were reached by these schools.[13] Until 1960 the South African government continued this German educational policy. The missions supplied the buildings and paid 50 percent of the cost of books, and the Union government paid the salaries of the teachers and supplied most school equipment. In 1960 the Bantu system of education used within the Republic was extended into South West Africa. The United Nations Committee on South West Africa viewed this action as a reinforcement of apartheid in the school system.[14] The educational standards of European and native schools are in no way equal, and the native educational system is not designed to prepare students for college or advanced

[13] Townsend, *Germany's Colonial Empire*, 292.
[14] South West Africa Committee, 16th Sess., Supp. No. 12 (A/4957, 1961), 25.

technical schools. Apparently, the South African government wishes to discourage higher education for the natives, especially if the natives must leave South African territory to acquire this education. Many natives who have been granted scholarships for study abroad have been denied passports.[15]

Nevertheless, some advancement in native education has been made in recent years. Since 1940 expenditures and enrollments in all educational categories have increased. In 1948 there were 16,106 non-European children of an estimated 43,700 enrolled in schools outside the police zone. Within the police zone reports from 1950 revealed that 9,161 non-European children of 30,700 were attending school. In the 1958-1959 period, total expenditures for education were £1,376,246, and the natives share was £251,303.[16] These figures represent a considerable increase over the 1940-1941 period when total expenditures were £165,032 and the native share was only £20,129.[17] In 1963, one out of nine non-Europeans in the territory supposedly was enrolled in school, and educational expenditures had risen to £500,000.[18]

South West African economy, never prosperous of its own accord and always heavily dependent upon South Africa, also reflects the application of the apartheid policy with natives limited to certain types of occupations and with bans on trade among whites and natives. The economic structure of South West Africa is less diverse than its ethnic composition. In recent years the economy has been subject to great fluctuations, chiefly because it is based upon export of a few primary goods. Drought also has contributed to this instability.

South West Africa's chief exports are animal hides and pelts, including karakul pelts, which are marketed as lambs' wool; other

[15] United Nations, General Assembly Resolutions, 14th Sess., Supp. No. 16, pp. 27-28.

[16] South West Africa Committee, 16th Sess., Supp. No. 12 (A/4957, 1961), 18-25.

[17] *Overseas Reference Book of the Union of South Africa*, ed. Julian Mockford (New York: Todd Publishing Co., 1945), 129.

[18] Alexander Steward, *South West Africa: The Sacred Trust* (Johannesburg: Da Gama Publications Limited, 1963), 31-32.

pastoral products, such as meat, butter, and wool; diamonds; and minerals, including vanadium, copper, and tin. Chief imports are foodstuffs, textiles, fibers, metals, manufactures, vehicles, and rubber products. In 1940 total imports were valued at £2,310,000, compared with exports of £3,680,000.[19] More than three-fourths of these exports consisted of agricultural products. Unofficial reports estimate 1959 exports at £45,000,000.[20] Exports in 1962 were reported at $131,600,000 and imports at $77,000,000. The per capita income per year is $164, but averages only $17 in the northern reserves.[21] South West Africa produces essentially the same products as does the Republic of South Africa; therefore, the economics are competitve rather than complementary, and South West Africa is not essential to the economic well-being of the Republic.

The territory's economy is closely integrated with that of the Republic of South Africa. No customs barriers exist between the two areas, and there is a free interchange of products and a transfer of duties collected on goods originally imported into one area and then shipped to the other. Prior to World War II, two-thirds of the total merchandise imported into South West Africa was either produced or handled in the Union of South Africa. During the war this dependence was increased. In 1948 the Union received 25 percent of South West Africa's exports and supplied nearly 67 percent of its imports. South West Africa's trade constituted little more than 2 percent of the Union's total foreign trade, 45 percent of South West Africa's trade was with the Union.[22] The rail, harbor, postal, telegraph, and telephone systems are also integrated with those of the Union.

The administration of the South West African mandate has

[19] United Nations, *Statistical Yearbook*, 1948, p. 315. Separate trade statistics on South West Africa have not been reported since this date.
[20] South West Africa Committee, 15th Sess., Supp. No. 12 (A/4464, 1960), 32.
[21] A *Handbook of African Affairs*, ed. Helen Kitchen (New York: pub. for the African-American Institute by Frederick A. Praeger, 1964), 150.
[22] United Nations, *Statistical Papers: Direction of International Trade*, 1961, pp. 271-74.

not been a profitable economic venture for the Republic of South Africa. Prior to 1927 the territory had a surplus of receipts over expenditures. A world depression, a series of droughts, and poor financial management brought indebtedness to the territory. As of 1957 South West Africa owed the Union £1,902,726 in loans and interest. However, this figure represents a considerable decrease in indebtedness over the previous ten years. The South Africa Railways Administration, which operates the South West African lines and seaports, also has a claim of £16,608,800 against the mandate. The administration maintains that it has lost that much in the operation of the lines since 1922. However, total South West African assets are £22,779,336 in excess of liabilities.[23] During the past few years the area has had a balanced budget.

The policy of apartheid or separate development also limits employment opportunities for natives. The United Nations' Committee on South West Africa concluded that opportunities open to non-Europeans are, on the whole, limited to the subordinate field of low-paid, unskilled labor in European enterprises and homes. This forces most African people to rely largely on subsistence agriculture and stockraising in the reserves.[24]

The South African government consistently has denied that the provisions of its Colour Bar Act have been applied to the South West Africa mandate. In 1928, A. J. Werth, South African representative to the League of Nations' Permanent Mandate Commission, said that a color bar was observed in practice, but that it was purely temporary and would continue only until the native had advanced sufficiently to be able to undertake responsible work, such as driving a motor car or working an engine.[25] These same types of statements are made by Republic officials today, almost forty years later.

[23] South West Africa Committee, 15th Sess., Supp. No. 12 (A/4464, 1960), 32.
[24] South West Africa Committee, 16th Sess., Supp. No. 12 (A/4957, 1961), 15.
[25] League of Nations, Permanent Mandates Commission, *Minutes*, 14th Sess., 23rd meeting.

Because industry in South West Africa is controlled by the European population, the only form of industry in which natives can invest is livestock production. Since the supplies of water and grass are limited, it is important that the number of livestock be restricted. During periods of drought some European farmers dismiss their native workers because the farm will not support both the cattle of the farmer and of the tenant. In 1958 it was estimated that there were seven and one-half million cattle within the police zone with Europeans owning five and one-half million.[26] Unofficial reports indicate that recent droughts have caused the loss of 90 percent of native livestock.[27]

Generally, the non-European seems to have accepted his lowly status as a mater of course. This acceptance of an inferior and exploited position is not likely to continue, however, because the South West African native is beginning to question and to reject his present position and is becoming politically aware and politically active.

Violence within South West Africa thus far has been minimal, but there is no guarantee that this will continue to be true. Unless the South African leaders make some concessions to the natives, violence is likely. As a result of uprisings and other troublesome signs, the Republic government apparently has reinforced its police and troops in South West Africa. A South West African spokesman told the United Nations that four new military bases and three new police stations had been constructed in South West Africa.[28]

The policy of apartheid has been the most criticized aspect of South African administration in South West Africa. Can the Europeans maintain by force, or by any other means, this policy in a territory where they are outnumbered eight to one, where

[26] South West Africa Committee, 15th Sess., Supp. No. 12 (A/4464, 1960), 33.

[27] South West Africa Committee, 16th Sess., Supp. No. 12 (A/4957, 1961), 15-16.

[28] United Nations, Fourth Committee Records, 16th Sess., I (Nov. 20, 1961), 376-80.

their economic stakes are not high, where their legal right even to be there is questioned, where African nationalism is growing, and where the moral support of the world is with the oppressed natives? Europeans must answer this question and answer it soon.

Originally under the supervision of the League of Nations, South West Africa's administration of the mandate since the demise of the League has been supervised by the United Nations.[29] Republic officials, however, have resisted the authority of the United Nations in reviewing and directing the governing of South West Africa. Under both systems of control the native has had little voice in the management of the territorial government.

The body most closely associated with League supervision was the Permanent Mandates Commission, a group of experts who were nominated by the League Council and who served as individuals rather than as government representatives. The commission was the liaison between the League Council and the mandatory government, and its functions were to advise the Council and to gather information concerning the mandate.

The administering power was required to submit annual reports and to forward written petitions to the Permanent Mandates Commission, and a representative of the mandatory government, who was expected to answer any question on the subject under consideration, always appeared before the commission during the examination of reports. No petitioners appeared before the commission, and no investigators were sent to the mandate. The United Nations Trusteeship System differs from the League's mandates system in both these procedures.

Under the mandates agreements any dispute relating to the interpretation and application of the mandate between the mandatory and another member of the League which could not be settled by negotiation would be submitted to the Permanent Court of International Justice. During the existence of the League no dispute concerning the Union's mandate agreement was submitted to the court. The United Nations, however, has frequently

[29] See Chs. II, III, and V.

requested rulings from the International Court concerning the South West Africa mandate.

The powers of supervision accorded to United Nations Trusteeship System are somewhat greater than those held by the League. The Trusteeship Council is composed of government representatives and it is more highly political than the League's commission. The increased power and changed composition of the Trusteeship Council are a partial explanation for South Africa's refusal to recognize the U.N. jurisdiction in the South West Africa dispute.

In the forty-five years of Union rule the Republic and South West Africa have become closely associated. Under the League mandate, South West Africa was to be governed as an integral part of the Union of South Africa, and Union laws were to be applied throughout the mandate. Prior to 1920 the mandate was under military occupation, but in that year the governor-general of the Union was given authority to do all such things as may be proper and expedient for giving effect to the mandate.[30] In actuality, the governor-general did not exercise these powers, and control was in the hands of the administrator, appointed by the Union government. Also, in 1920 through 1925 a series of laws was initiated which set up much of the administrative machinery of South West Africa and which allowed application of many Union laws to the mandate.

It was not until the 1925 constitution that any resident of South West Africa had a voice in the government. This constitution established new government machinery and provided for limited political participation for the European population—to all adult Europeans who would accept British citizenship. The native population could not vote, but one member of the Advisory Council was appointed to represent native interests.

The Constitutional Act of 1925 established the Executive Committee, the Advisory Council, and the Legislative Assembly for

---

[30] Quincy Wright, *Mandates Under the League of Nations* (Chicago: University of Chicago Press, 1930), 424.

South West Africa. The Executive Committee was composed of the administrator and four members elected by the Legislative Assembly. This group could advise on any matter within the ordinance-making sphere of the Legislative Assembly.

The Advisory Council was composed of the administrator, the four members of the Executive Committee, and three members appointed by the administrator with the approval of the governor-general. The Advisory Council consulted with the administration on those matters reserved from legislation by the Assembly, the preparation of the financial estimates, the assent of ordinances passed by the Assembly, and any matter referred to it by the administrator.

The Legislative Assembly consisted of eighteen members, twelve elected by the ballot of registered voters; the remaining six were nominated by the administrator with the approval of the governor-general. Legislative terms were five years, and sessions were held at least once during each fiscal year. The Legislative Assembly could not pass laws on the following matters without the consent of the governor-general of the Union: (1) native affairs; (2) mines and minerals; (3) railways and harbors; (4) the public service; (5) constitution, jurisdiction and procedure of courts of justice; (6) posts, telegraphs, and telephones; (7) military organization; (8) movement and operations of the Defense Force of the Union of South Africa; (9) immigration; (10) customs and excise; (11) currency and banking. The following areas were also reserved, but the Legislative Assembly could be granted extended powers into these spheres upon the recommendation of a two-thirds vote of its membership: (1) police force; (2) civil aviation; (3) education; (4) land and agricultural bank; (5) government land.

The powers granted to the Legislative Assembly were not great. In effect, the administrator controlled all forms of government activity except defense, and police (which were combined with the Union force), and railways and harbors (which were controlled directly by the Union government). Acting under the authority of the administrator was a secretary for South West Africa, who also served as accounting officer and chief native commissioner.[31] Any ordinance passed by the Assembly had to be presented to the administrator for agreement. If the administrator withheld his approval, he could refer the ordinance back to the Assembly or reserve it for consideration by the governor-general. By resolution the Legislative Assembly could recommend to the governor-general or to the administrator the issuance of a proclamation on any reserved subject. The estimates of expenditure for the territory were submitted to the Assembly which could reduce or omit items. However, if it rejected or failed to pass the necessary provision of money for the ordinary services of the administration, or if it rejected an ordinance imposing any tax which the administrator had certified to be necessary for the purposes of general administration, the governor-general could, on report from the administrator, make the appropriation by proclamation.[23]

The administration also included a secretariat, and branches of the department of native affairs, works, agriculture, education, lands, mines, posts, prisons, and public works. The South West African civil service was staffed primarily by Union public servants.

This constitution provided a poor framework for building the political participation of the native and democratic self-governing processes. For the native, who has an eight to one majority, it did nothing. He could neither vote nor hold office. His interests were represented by a man who was selected by Europeans and who sat on a committee with no power.

The basic provisions of this 1925 Constitutional Act remained unaltered until the Union Parliament passed the South West African Affairs Act in 1949, which virtually made South West Africa a fifth province of the Union of South Africa. This brought serious criticism from United Nations members. The major provision of the bill granted representation to white South West Africans in the Union Parliament. This change must be interpreted as a move to incorporate the mandate into the Union, as

[31] *South West Africa and the Union*, 39-40.
[32] "Progress of Government," *South-West Africa Annual*, 1945, pp. 17-23.

the relationship of South West Africa to the Union became little different from the relationship of the four provinces of the Union to their own central government.

Under this act the European population of South West Africa elects six representatives to the Union's House of Assembly. Two senators are elected for ten years by an electoral college composed of members of the Legislative Assembly and the South West African members of Parliament. The governor-general also appoints two senators one of whom is chosen from his "acquaintance with the reasonable wants and wishes of the colored races of the territory." The Advisory Council, on which the natives had a spokesman, was replaced by the Executive Committee.

The Legislative Assembly retained its eighteen members, and its powers theoretically were increased, because it was granted the authority to deal with education, land and agricultural bank, Crown lands, and mines and minerals. Control of the police organization and civil aviation were permanently restricted from consideration by the Assembly. All powers of legislation which had been vested in the governor-general in 1920 were transferred to the Union Parliament. With only one exception the Union Parliament is absolutely supreme over the Legislative Assembly of South West Africa. While Pairliament may override any Assembly ordinance, it cannot extend a direct tax upon the peoples of the Union to the territory.[33] Obviously, this act did not broaden the political participation of the native population; its purpose was to make one additional step toward annexation of the mandate.[34]

South West Africa's court system has jurisdiction only over the European population, because the natives supposedly have their own legal system. In civil cases the High Court is composed of a single judge, and in criminal cases two assessors, who must be advocates or magistrates, sit with the judge. No juries are used. The Circuit Court is similar in organization to the High Court.

[33] See Union of South Africa, House of Assembly Debates, Feb. 21, 1949, and "The Modified Constitution of South West Africa," South-West Africa Annual, 1951, pp. 9-13.
[34] See Ch. III.

Appeal from both these courts goes to the appellate division of the Supreme Court of South Africa. The lowest division of the court system is the Magistrates' Court. This judicial organization has been in effect since 1920. The law applied in South West Africa consists of Roman Dutch law; certain portions of German law; and acts, ordinances, and proclamations of the Union government and of the Legislative Assembly of South West Africa.[35]

Local government in South West Africa is a complex and confused process with the application of apartheid adding to this complexity. In theory, separate development means that in predominantly native areas natives have their own governing boards or councils, the authority to make some ordinances governing their own territory, and their own court system which applies tribal law. The Europeans have a similar arrangement in the European areas. Presumably, each racial group pursues its own development at its desired speed and in the direction it prefers. Under this system the natives would not be forced to advance at a rate too fast for their adjustment, and the Europeans would not be held back.

Prior to 1954, native affairs were under the control of the administrator of the territory, who was responsible to the Union government. Native affairs then were administered by the Union's minister of native affairs.[36] This change in policy was interpreted by many U.N. members as an attempt by the Union government to associate South West African native policy even more closely with that of the Union.

Within the police zone the magistrate acts as native commissioner. Each reserve has a welfare officer who is responsible for the administration of native reserve regulations. Law provides that he will be assisted by a native reserve board composed of the headmen of the tribe and up to six additional native members elected by the natives, yet few of the native boards, councils, or

[35] *South West Africa and the Union,* 40-41.
[36] South West Africa Committee, 10th Sess., Supp. No. 12 (A/2913, 1955), 30.

courts provided by law have been established,[37] and the natives are rarely consulted about policy even at this level.

Native townships within European urban areas are the responsibility of the local authorities. In theory, each native township has an advisory board consisting of not less than three natives resident in each township.[38] In the European or white townships and districts some councils have been organized. These councils date back to the period of German rule, and they were reestablished by the Union in the early 1920's. Usually, half the members are appointed by the administrator and half are elected, and most have an advisory function only.[39]

The two major European political parties of South West Africa are the leading parties of the Republic of South Africa, although the strength of parties composed primarily of natives has been increasing. The ruling Nationalist party was formed in 1912 by General James Hertzog after a split with Generals Louis Botha and Jan Christian Smuts over the Union's entrance into World War I. Hertzog wished to remain neutral, and he opposed the concept of Dutch cooperation with the British. His party represented a policy of Dutch supremacy which was symbolized by the use of Afrikaans.[40] The followers of Hertzog took the Union of South Africa out of the British Commonwealth and made South Africa a republic. The South African party of Botha and Smuts favored cooperation among the Europeans of South Africa and took a more international view on issues. Both parties have associated themselves to one degree or another with the policy of apartheid and with retaining control of South West Africa at almost any cost.

Likely, the various native groups which are springing up in South Africa and in South West Africa may hold more significance for the future than do the now-powerful European political parties. The largest native political organization in South West Africa is

[37] South West Africa Committee, 19.
[38] *South West Africa and the Union*, 64-66.
[39] *Overseas Reference Book*, 124.
[40] Afrikaans is the South African corruption of Dutch.

the South West Africa Political Organization (S.W.A.P.O.). Though membership of this group is not restricted because of race or religion, it is primarily a nonwhite organization. The South West Africa Political Organization, formerly called the Ovamboland People's Congress, desires democratic government established under United Nations supervision. A second group, with similar aims, is the South West Africa National Union (S.W.A. N.U.). The African National Congress and the Pan African Congress are also gaining support among the natives of the territory.[41]

S.W.A.P.O. claims a membership of 90,000 and S.W.A.N.U. lists 10,000.[42] Some observers fear that S.W.A.N.U., which is led by Fanuel Jairetunda Kozonguize and that S.W.A.P.O., which includes Sam Nujoma among its leaders, are supporters of the Communist Chinese line. The Chinese are urging the natives to oppose United Nations intervention and to take up arms and fight.[43] If South West Africa should become an ideological battleground for the Communist and non-Communist forces, this undoubtedly would paralyze U.N. actions. If the native should be won to Communism, then the western countries would be forced to back the white non-Communist minority. The near-unanimous support which the U.N. has given the South West African native would be split along Communist and non-Communist lines. It is unfortunate that South Africa officials have banned meetings of native parties, for this may force them to become more militant.[44]

It is obvious that the South African administration of South West Africa has done little to promote or to permit the political development of the inhabitants. This is especially the case with the native peoples. Some of the natives are becoming politically aware, and they are demanding greater participation in politics. While the majority of natives in South West Africa still manifest a docile acceptance of their conditions, the native African will

[41] "Political Parties Grow," *Africa Digest*, VIII (June, 1961), 247.
[42] *A Handbook of African Affairs*, 51.
[43] John K. Cooley, *East Wind Over Africa* (New York: Walker and Co., 1965), 88-89.
[44] "Meeting Banned," *Africa Digest*, X (Feb. 1963), 141.

not be content until white supremacy is abolished in all Africa. His attack has been centered on South West Africa because the territory possesses an international status. Through the United Nations, international machinery has been created to advance the welfare of the natives, and the administering power cannot protect itself from international inquiry by claiming that its domestic jurisdiction has been violated. The Africans have been joined in this struggle by the peoples of Asia, who also know the effects of colonialism and racial discrimination. Aside from the moral and legal merits of the South West Africa case, the cold-war struggle for the uncommitted masses of the world has forced all major nations to align themselves with the South West African native.

TWO:

THE INTERNATIONAL MANDATE

As a part of the post-World War I settlement, the Union of South Africa acquired a League of Nations mandate for South West Africa. This 1919 agreement ended a period of harsh German rule of the territory which had begun when Otto von Bismark declared South West Africa a German protectorate in 1884 and then annexed it formally in 1892. German rule was marked by economic loss and by native revolt, and the German administration did almost nothing to further the economic and political interests of the natives. German policy in South West Africa was designed to exploit cheap native labor and to provide the homeland with additional resources. They did not plan to establish permanent colonies in the territory and therefore were not concerned with long-term capital improvements. Conversely, the South Africans intended to colonize parts of South West Africa for white inhabitation, but as the Germans, they came primarily to exploit the natives. The implications which can be drawn from both colonial policies are that neither gave proper attention to the basic needs of the native majority.

South African claims to the former German colony were strong, so strong, in fact that the government under Prime Minister Louis Botha and General Jan Christian Smuts pushed for outright annexation. Smuts apparently had fallen under the influence of imperialism, for he not only asked the Paris Peace Conference to grant his government the right to annex South West Africa but he later also talked of union with Southern Rhodesia, Basutoland, Bechuanaland, and Swaziland.

South Africa's chief claim to South West Africa was military conquest, and the circumstances under which the South African government had entered World War I strengthened this claim.

The Union of South Africa entered the war and launched an attack against South West Africa only after a period of heated debate and numerous instances of open rebellion. Many of the Boers and the Germans within the Union wished to remain neutral, and the Dutch settlers had not forgotten their defeat to the British in the Boer War. The Boer government of Botha and Smuts, however, felt that there were a number of reasons for the Union to join the side of the British in World War I. Naturally, they argued that as a part of the British Empire the Union of South Africa was constitutionally obligated to enter the war. Also, Botha and Smuts felt cooperation with the British would unify the white population of the Union. Additionally, the presence of the Germans in South West Africa was a potential threat to the Union. Finally, there was the prospect of gaining control of South West Africa.

On August 10, 1914, the South African government sent an expeditionary force to South West Africa.[1] Eleven months later the main German force in the territory surrendered. It then became a political necessity for Botha and Smuts to show a tangible gain from the war, because they had been forced to fight some of their own people while aiding the British. If they failed to acquire South West Africa, they might be overthrown by the opposition party, the Nationalists. At the Paris Peace Conference Smuts stressed his country's loyalty to the British and the Union army's military contributions to the allied victory.

In an earlier era military conquest might have secured international recognition of the right to rule the conquered area. Now, however, because of the United States' President Woodrow Wilson's policies of no annexations, self-determination, and the impartial adjustment of all colonial claims, the old rationalé of the victor's power over the vanquished no longer was an adequate justification for taking away German colonies. This justification

[1] Eric A. Walker, *A History of Southern Africa* (New York: Longman's Green and Co., 1957), 59.

came to rest largely upon German misrule and misuse of her possessions.

The decision to deprive Germany of her colonial possessions had been made long before the delegations gathered at Paris. Smuts' job, as chief spokesman for the Union at Paris, was to convince the delegates that his country should be permitted to annex South West Africa. On January 24, 1919, Smuts presented his case to a conference committee, stressing the Union's contribution to the war effort and the unfitness of the Germans as colonial administrators. Smuts also emphasized the contiguity of the territories. Geographically, they were one, and the area was strategically vital to the defense of the Union. South West Africa would have been annexed long before if the Imperial government had not regarded it as an economic liability. South West Africa differed from Germany's other African possessions. The Cameroons, Togoland, and East Africa all were tropical and valuable, while South West Africa was suitable only for stock herding and therefore could not be developed apart from the Union.

Thirdly, Smuts argued, a white community in South Africa had been established for two or three centuries. It had done its best to give a form of self-government to three million natives, and its policy had been tested and found good. This policy should be applied to the natives of South West Africa,[2] Smuts continued.

This reference to the white policies of the Union was made in a casual manner and stressed the benefits which could result for the natives of South West Africa. However, the past forty-five years of South African administration in the area make one wonder if Smuts failed to give proper emphasis to this point. Parts of South West Africa were suitable for European settlement, and Union administration of the area would mean a larger territory under direct European control. Under the Immigration Quota Act of 1930, as amended in 1931, immigration into South West

[2] David Hunter Miller, *My Diary at the Conference of Paris*, 20 vols. (New York: Printed for the author by the Appeal Printing Co., 1924), XIV, 26-27.

Africa was limited to nationals of the British Commonwealth (no nonwhites), France, Austria, Italy, the Scandinavian countries, Holland, Spain, Portugal, Switzerland, and the United States.[3] It has been government policy to encourage white settlement of the area. The United Nations Committee on South West Africa noted that no nonwhites immigrated into the territory between 1945 and 1949.[4] Almost inescapable is the conclusion that the chief motive in the Republic of South Africa's refusal to place South West Africa under the United Nations Trusteeship System is the extension of apartheid and the maintenance of a buffer zone against Black Africa. The resulting situation is ironic: South Africa's racial policy is the chief reason the world would deny them the territory.

At the time of the Paris Peace Conference South Africa was, and still is, the most logical administrator for South West Africa. The South Africans possess adequate resources and technology to develop the territory, and their geographic proximity would insure adequate defense.

The South African government did not convince the Paris Peace Conference that South West Africa should be annexed, and the government was forced to accept a C mandate for the territory. If Wilson had not announced his Fourteen Points program, which included the concepts of self-determination and no annexation, South Africa and all the other victorious powers likely would have annexed the colonies they had conquered during the war. The Fourteen Points undoubtedly were issued partially in response to Lenin's charges of capitalistic imperialism. If the democratic nations wished to disprove Bolshevik propaganda, they could hardly make an exception of South West Africa. However, the fact that the South Africans sought annexation is significant. Although the Union incurred international obligations by accept-

[3] Ansu Kuman, "South-West Africa Under the Mandatory System," *Africa Quarterly* II (Oct.-Dec., 1962), 161.
[4] United Nations, Report of the Committee on South West Africa, 9th Sess., Supp. No. 14 (A/2666, 1954), 28.

ing the mandate, the subsequent Union governments have acted as if outright annexation had been granted. In a speech at Windhoek in 1920, Smuts said that the mandate was little but annexation.[5]

Smuts and leaders of successive governments have referred to statements and events at the Paris Peace Conference to justify this virtual annexation. For example, these spokesmen quote Woodrow Wilson as having told the Council of Ten that a mandate agreement might lead to union with the mandatory power. This statement is out of context and does not reveal Wilson's true intention. What Wilson actually said in his January 27, 1919, statement concerning mandates was: "The purpose was to serve the people in undeveloped parts, to safeguard them against abuses such as had occurred under German administration and such as might be found under other administrations. Further where people and territories were underdeveloped, to assure their development, so that, when the time came, their interests, as they saw them, might qualify them to express a wish as to their ultimate relations—perhaps lead them to desire their union with the mandatory power."[6]

Another statement made at the Paris Peace Conference has been used by the Union government to justify the closest possible association between South Africa and South West Africa. In Wilson's Third Paris Draft of February 2, 1919, C mandates were to be administered "as if integral portions thereof."[7] In a meeting of the Commission on the League on February 8, 1919, Smuts presented an amendment which also contained this clause. Baron Makino of Japan suggested that the "if" be stricken from the draft, and this proposal was approved by the commission.[8]

[5] J. I. Goldblatt, *The Mandated Territory of South West Africa in Relation to the United Nations* (Cape Town: C. Struik, 1961), 10.

[6] Ray Stannard Baker, *Woodrow Wilson and World Settlement*, 3 vols. (Garden City: Doubleday, Page and Co., 1922), I, 262.

[7] David Hunter Miller, *The Drafting of the Covenant*, 2 vols. (New York· G. P. Putnam's Sons, 1928), I, 152.

[8] Miller, *Drafting of the Covenant*, 273-75.

Smuts himself later referred to the elimination of the "if" as evidence of practical sovereignty over the C mandates.[9] Further evidence of Smuts' position on South West Africa was revealed in a speech he made before the South African Parliament on July 13, 1925: "I should have preferred the two countries more closely linked up at this stage. When I urge this it may be said that I am working in favor of the annexation of Southwest Africa to the Union; but I am not. I do not think it is necessary for us to annex Southwest Africa to the Union. The mandate for me is enough. It gives the Union such complete power of sovereignty, not only administrative, but legislative, that we need not ask for anything more."[10]

Regardless of Smuts' real opinion concerning annexation, he went to the San Francisco Conference in 1945 to seek again the annexation of South West Africa. For a man who supposedly did not want annexation, Smuts tried hard to secure it.

Ironically, Smuts, who sought annexation, was as instrumental as anyone in the establishment of the League of Nations Mandates system. Scholars differ as to whether Smuts or Wilson made the greater contribution to the mandates scheme, but most agree that Smuts played a major role. Had Smuts realized that the mandates system would be applied to South West Africa, he might not have been so enthusiastic in promoting it.

On December 16, 1918, Smuts published his proposals for the League of Nations and for a mandates system under the title of *The League of Nations: A Practical Suggestion.* Smuts' philosophy embodied principles of internationalism and provincialism which were upon occasions contradictory. This conflict is revealed by Smuts' acceptance of the concepts of self-determination and no annexation as the basis for a colonial settlement, so long as they were not applied to areas his country wished to control. Smuts was a leading statesman who sought international approval for his

[9] Quincy Wright, *Mandates Under the League of Nations* (Chicago: University of Chicago Press, 1930), 581.

[10] Quoted from Van Rees in League of Mandates, Permanent Mandates Commission, *Minutes*, 9th Sess., 5th meeting.

and his nation's policy. As long as he remained in power, he asked the League and the United Nations to sanction his government's action in South West Africa.

Smuts proposed a mandates system which would be applied to certain areas formerly under the control of Russia, Austria-Hungary, and Turkey. The disposal of these colonies would be based on Wilson's principles of no annexation, the right of self-determination, the right of the people to appeal to the League against a breach of the mandate, and the open-door policy. Smuts did not include the German territories in his suggestion because he felt the German areas in the Pacific and in Africa were inhabited by barbarians who could not possibly govern themselves and that it would be impracticable to apply to them any ideas of political self-determination in the European sense.[11] British Prime Minister Winston Churchill said that Smuts never thought the mandates system was suited to the regions conquered by the various British Dominions. Least of all did he expect it to be applied to South West Africa, which the Union government intended to annex. That would be carrying a sound principle too far.[12]

The mandates system did not take the exact form Wilson would have preferred, but he was successful in having it applied to the German colonies. Direct annexation was not feasible, but a mandatory system which made few concessions to the administering nations was unacceptable to the conquering powers. As is the case with most international agreements, compromise was a necessity. Smuts suggested a compromise which with the addition of a few amendments was adopted by the conference. His proposal called for division of the mandates into three distinct categories (later referred to as A, B, and C mandates) based on the following considerations: (1) the stage of development of the people, (2) the geographical situation of the territory, and (3) the economic conditions of the area. For example, the peoples of the central

---

[11] Jan Christian Smuts, *The League of Nations: A Practical Suggestion* (New York: Hodder and Stoughton, 1918), 12-15.

[12] Winston Churchill, *The Aftermath* (New York: Charles Scribner's Sons, 1929), 150.

portions of Africa were at such a stage of development that the mandatory must be responsible for administering the territory subject to conditions which would prohibit abuses such as the slave trade, the arms traffic, and the liquor traffic, and would prevent military training of the natives for other than police purposes. Such territories as South West Africa and certain islands of the South Pacific, which, because of their sparse population, their small size, their remoteness from the centers of civilization, or their geographical contiguity to the mandatory state could best be administered under the laws of the mandatory state as an integral portion of that state, subject to the above-mentioned safeguards in the interest of the indigenous population.[13]

The mandates, established under article twenty-two of the League Covenant and assigned to the administering powers by the Supreme Council of the Conference on May 6, 1919, were carved from three former parts of the Ottoman Empire and seven former overseas possessions of Germany. These ten areas were administered as fifteen mandates, and all former German areas were classified as either B or C mandates.

For a number of reasons South Africa though the classification of South West Africa as a C mandate was an attractive compromise. The area could be governed as an integral part of the Union, and laws of the Union not in conflict with the stated provisions of the mandate agreement could be applied to South West Africa. Under this provision the Union of South Africa has felt justified in extending its immigration and racial policies into the territory. Also, under the C mandate agreement the administering power did not have to maintain the open-door policy, allowing South Africa to establish a tariff union between the two areas and to extend the British preferential system to South West Africa. Since the C territories were the most backward, it was likely that these mandates would be of the longest duration. Smuts apparently felt that the C mandate agreement was as close to annexation as he would get at the time.

13 Miller, *Drafting of the Covenant*, 110.

Many important questions were left unanswered in the League agreement and remain unanswered today. Precisely, what does promoting to the utmost the material and moral well-being and the social progress of the inhabitants mean? How far would the administering power be expected to go in fulfilling these principles? What would be the consequences if an administrator violated the agreement? After the League expired, were these provisions still binding? When did the sovereignty of South Africa reside? These answers were not spelled out. The wording of the C mandates was deliberately ambiguous, designed to give the mandatory extensive powers, but not sovereignty over the territories. The vagueness surrounding the mandates system was not the result of carelessness, but was a reflection of a lack of agreement among the parties concerned. The intent of the agreements was clear, but enforcement to a large degree rested upon the willingness of the powers directly concerned to act in a responsible manner.

THREE:

CRITICISM OF SOUTH AFRICAN POLICY

Although the chief criticisms of Union administration of the South West Africa mandate made by both the League of Nations and the United Nations have pertained to native policy and annexation attempts, these criticisms have differed significantly. Recent international trends opposed to colonialism and racial discrimination have made the South West Africa issue a political and moral one, and worldwide opinion will not sanction a regime so anachronistic in light of modern political and social philosophy. The European residents of South Africa will not accept this fact, believing they are preserving a superior culture; they might have been wiser had they shared rather than preserved their culture, intellect, wealth, and power.

The change in attitudes on discrimination and colonialism is reflected clearly in the change between opinions expressed by the League and those expressed by members of the United Nations. The United Nations has been far more critical of South African policy, reflecting this post-World War II liberalism. The different composition of the U.N. from that of the League also accounts for the sterner criticism. Unlike the League Mandates Commission,, the United Nations Trusteeship Council is composed of government representatives and is, therefore, more political. Its views are the views of governments, not of individuals. The League was composed predominately of nations with white majority populations; the United Nations is not. The League contained a large percentage of colonial powers, whereas the United Nations General Assembly has a large majority which is anticolonial. The large Afro-Asian bloc in the United Nations, which is highly concerned with racial and colonial issues, has led the attack against Union policies and is finding increasing support among all members. The South West Africa case is becoming more and more an emotional issue with the opinions of all parties concerned based not only upon political and legal issues, but also upon moral principle. Where a moral principle is involved, it is difficult to be patient and to compromise.

Another reason for the impatience within the United Nations is that forty-five years of Union rule has done little for the natives. When the League stopped functioning in 1939, the Union's administration had been in operation less than twenty years. German rule had created many problems, and accelerated change would have been disruptive, so the members of the League were willing to give South Africa additional time. The members of the United Nations do not feel that time is the answer and that too little has been done.

Although the Union promised to promote to the utmost the material and moral well-being and the social progress of the inhabitants, the native majority has been denied economic, social, political, and educational opportunity. Political apartheid has meant that natives have had no right to vote on any important issue or to hold public office. Financial apartheid, according to the United Nations Committee on South West Africa, has meant exclusion of non-Europeans in every culturally relevant field, including education, technical and professional training, provision of credit, marketing arrangements, and disposal of land and mineral rights.[1]

The League's most severe censure of the South African administration came as a result of two native uprisings, in 1922 and in 1925. The League also sharply criticized native labor policies as outlined by the Union. The first of these revolts erupted among the Bondelswart tribe in the southern portion of the territory as a result of a tax imposed upon dogs. Since the Bondelswarts were hunters, dogs were a necessity. The tax had been imposed because the natives, though poverty-stricken, had refused to work for white farmers. Violence was touched off by the natives' refusal to

[1] United Nations, Report of the Committee on South West Africa, 15th Sess., Supp. No. 12 (A/4464, 1960), 32.

surrender to police authorities Abraham Morris, a Bondelswart leader who had returned to the reserve without proper authorization. The Union government ordered the reserve bombarded by planes in an attack which lasted nine hours and killed more than one hundred men, women, and children. South Africa also charged a number of native leaders with high treason.[2]

The League of Nations Mandates Commission concluded by a vote of eight to five that the trouble was due fundamentally to native grievances arising from legislation and administrative action in behalf of the white settlers and, more immediately, to the mistakes of the administration after the situation had become serious. The chairman of the commission, Marquis Theodoli, stated that while the mandatory's first duty should be to the natives, in this case it had "pursued a policy of force rather than of persuasion and further that the policy had always been conceived and applied in the interest of the colonists rather than in the interests of the natives." The commission could not approve such a method of imposing forced labor for the benefit of private individuals.[3]

The Rehoboth Revolt of 1925 had less serious consequences for the natives. The Rehoboths had enjoyed some degree of self-rule under old treaty rights, and General Botha had promised them during World War I that these privileges would be preserved. When the mandate was created, the Rehoboths formed a state within a state. It was not clear to what degree the tribe would cooperate with the mandatory power. There was also a dispute between the tribe and the administration over the extent of the Rehoboth reserve, and the mandatory decided to prove its authority by enforcing an unpopular law which required the natives to have their cattle branded by the magistrates. Under this ordinance the natives had to pay thirty shillings for brandirons which they could not keep. When the natives took up arms, the administrator once

[2] Freda White, *Mandates* (London: Jonathan Cape, LTD., 1926), 136-37.
[3] Quincy Wright, *Mandates Under the League of Nations* (Chicago: University of Chicago Press, 1930), 209-10.

again summoned white troops and airplanes, but this time the natives surrendered without bloodshed.[4]

In 1924 before the revolt the Rehoboths had petitioned the League, saying that their rights had been denied. The Union government had delayed in forwarding and commenting upon this petition. The Union's defense for this delay was that the telegram had been unintelligible and had been held, pending elucidation from the senders. The Permanent Mandate Commission said the mandatory power was remiss in dealing with the Rehoboth's grievances, and it noted that while the case was pending, the mandatory had treated the natives as if they had been wrong.[5]

Only one riot of any consequence has occurred in recent years—in Windhoek on December 10, 1959. The underlying cause was the attempted relocation of 170 native families to a site in Katuturo, just outside Windhoek. The new location was designed according to the new regulation that there must be at least a 500-yard buffer zone between white and nonwhite settlements. Charging that the relocation would promote apartheid, the families refused to move. They also claimed residence at the new site would mean higher rents and use of bus transportation to get to and from their jobs. When authorities forced the families to move, the South West African National Union and the Ovamboland Congress organized a boycott of buses, beer halls, and movies run by the city. Union police opened fire on the natives, and in the ensuing riot twelve natives were killed and forty were injured. Eight white policemen also were wounded.[6] The United Nations General Assembly condemned the police for firing on the natives and demanded punishment of those responsible for the native deaths.[7]

Both the League and the United Nations have been critical of

[4] White, *Mandates*, 140-41.

[5] League of Nations, Permanent Mandates Commission, *Minutes*, 14th Sess., 7th meeting.

[6] "Windhoek Crisis," *Africa Digest*, VII (February, 1960), 130-31.

[7] United Nations, General Assembly Resolutions, 15th Sess., Supp. No. 16, Res. 1567(XV).

the Union's labor and financial policies toward the natives. For example, in 1928 the League's Permanent Mandates Commission noted a statement by the administrator that the Colour Bar Act of the Union had been applied to South West Africa, at least in employment practices under the administration and in the railways. The commission considered that this act, which limited the occupations open to native and colored workers and thus placed them at a disadvantage to white workers, was contrary to principles expressed in the mandate. The commission also concluded that the Union had not set adequate safeguards for the health of the natives who worked in the mines.[8] More recent studies by the U.N. show that these conditions have not improved.

In 1936 the Union government appointed a commission composed of Mr. Justice Van den Heever, Mr. Justice Van Zyl, and Dr. J. E. Holloway to study the effectiveness of South African administration in South West Africa. This commission concluded that while the Union government had discharged the primary functions of government, such as establishing law and order, it had been a failure and should be abolished. The Van Zyl Commission noted that appropriations were inadequate to provide needed educational, medical, and general improvements for the natives. Moreover, the group disclosed that native appropriations were the first to be cut in times of financial hardship.[9] Both the League and the United Nations have echoed the remarks of the Van Zyl Commission, but the Union of South Africa has refused to act upon these criticisms. The Europeans of South Africa and South West Africa feel the natives should pay for their own development, but it is difficult for the natives to pay for these services when they are kept at the bottom of the economic ladder.

While the League of Nations did little but talk, its criticisms of Union administration were becoming more serious. Mrs. V. M. L. Ballinger, a liberal member of the Union House of Assembly, said that during the last years of the League's existence

[8] Mandates Commission, 14th Sess., 23rd meeting.
[9] "The South West Africa Commission," *Round Table*, XXII (1936), 772-77.

there was growing anxiety in international circles over the Union's administration: "The last years of the Permanent Mandates Commission's existence were years in which the conduct of this mandate was the subject of very close enquiry and, if not specific criticisms, certainly implicit criticisms."[10]

Since unanimous resolutions passed by the League were considered binding, one might argue that the League was somewhat better equipped to take action against the mandatory power than the United Nations, but this argument is irrelevant. The League was still basically a white, colonial body. The Union of South Africa has cooperated less with the United Nations than it did with the League, but this disadvantage has been offset somewhat by the United Nations' broader powers of supervision. The U.N. has accepted oral petitions, sent observers to South West Africa, and established a special committee to supervise the administration of the mandate. Despite these greater powers, however, the U.N. has been no more successful than the League was. Neither body has resorted to economic and military sanctions, both confining their efforts to applying moral pressure. If a nation wishes to disregard resolutions passed by a two-thirds vote or those passed unanimously, it may do so. Short of establishing a world government, this will remain so. The leading world powers have been reluctant to take stronger actions in South West Africa because many other world problems pose a more immediate threat to international peace and security.

Although the League was critical of Union administration, it never suggested that the mandate should be removed from South African control. After years of heated debate, passage of more than sixty resolutions, and suggestions of a dozen compromises, many U.N. members felt that stronger measures were necessary. The Committee on South West Africa, which was created by the General Assembly in 1953 and charged with the responsibility of supervising the administration of South West Africa, gives in its 1961 report the opinion of these members concluding that the

[10] Union of South Africa, House of Assembly Debates, Feb. 23, 1949, cols. 1547-48.

current administration of South West Africa is based upon apartheid; that this form of administration constitutes a violation of the charter, the Covenant, and the mandate; that no plans for reform were revealed by the Union government; and that it is the overwhelming desire of the native population that the United Nations assume control of the territory. The committee recommended that the General Assembly consider voting sanctions against the Union, and if this failed, the U.N. should revoke the mandate and establish self-government in the territory.[11]

The importance of South Africa's racial policies in the South West Africa case cannot be overemphasized. The country might continue these policies in its own territory for an indefinite period, but the maintenance of these procedures in an international mandate is another matter. Many Union leaders have come to regard the South West Africa issue as a backdoor through which its domestic racial policies are aired publicly, and this point undoubtedly contains some truth. India, because of the treatment of Indian nationals within the Union, had an interest in the Union's racial policies, and the African and Asian states naturally resented apartheid. Russia and the Soviet bloc desired to influence favorably the anticolonial countries. Because their racial policy is being challenged, many Union nations both resent and fear U.N. intervention in the South West Africa case. Prime Minister J. G. Strijdom warned that if South West Africa came under United Nations jurisdiction, there would be no color distinction.[12] Prime Minister Daniel F. Malan said that the U.N. "wants to thrust down our throats a doctrine of equality between whites and non-whites. In the League of Nations we had to do with a reasonable body. The League trusted the Union and South West Africa. But the U.N.O. is quite another body."[13]

Certainly, other questions than the one of race are involved in

[11] United Nations, Report of the Special Committee for South West Africa, 17th Sess., Supp. No. 12 (A/5121, 1961), 6.

[12] "South African Prime Minister Says Mandate no Longer Exists," *Africa Digest*, III (October, 1955), 13.

[13] *New York Times*, Aug. 8, 1950, 16.

the South West Africa issue. If, however, the issues were purely legal, political, economic, or geographic, the Union government would have few problems in bringing its policies into accord with international principles as expressed through the League of Nations and the United Nations.

The second aspect of Union administration which has been most criticized has been the tendency of the Union government to act as if it had actually acquired sovereignty over South West Africa. The policy of the Union governments in this respect has been relatively consistent. Smuts tried to secure recognition of annexation at the Paris Peace Conference in 1918 and at the San Francisco Conference in 1945. All governments of South Africa have acted as if these efforts had been far more successful than they actually were.

As early as 1920 Smuts stated that the mandate was little else but annexation. In 1922 the Railways and Harbours Act gave the Union "full dominion" over the railways and harbors of South West Africa. The League commission regarded this an incorrect term in reference to the control of property within a mandate.[14] In 1923 a legal issue resulting from the Bondelswart Revolt was brought before the appellate division of the Supreme Court of South Africa. The defendant, Jacobus Christian, maintained that he could not be found guilty of high treason against the Union of South Africa because that country did not have sovereignty over South West Africa. In *Rex v. Christian*, the majority held that while South Africa did not possess full sovereignty, it had adequate authority to bring a charge of high treason.[15] The decision itself was not a subject of debates, but the arguments of some of the justices in defense of the decision brought comments from League members. For example, Justice De Villiers stated that sovereignty in South West Africa resided in the Union of South Africa which had full power of administration and legisla-

[14] Mandates Commission, 14th Sess., 12th meeting.
[15] Aaron M. Margalith, *The International Mandates* (Baltimore: John Hopkins Press, 1930), 186-88.

tion (limited only in certain definite respects) and does not recognize the sovereignty of any person or body in the territory. Judge Wessels wrote that once the League of Nations had handed the territory over to the Union government, the League as such had no right or power to dictate to the mandatory power what laws should be established in South West Africa and how the territory should be governed.[16]

A 1926 treaty between the Union of South Africa and Portugal stated that South Africa "possesses sovereignty" in the mandated area.[17] The Permanent Mandates Commission stated that: "All these facts—certain silences as well as certain statements—had necessarily, throughout past years, confirmed the Commission in its view—a view which it had regretted having to form, and which dated perhaps from the day when it learned that General Smuts, then the Prime Minister, had stated publicly, in September 1920, that in his eyes C mandates constituted a situation almost equivalent to annexation."[18]

In its 1936 report to the League the Union government stated that the administration of South West Africa as a fifth province of the Union would not conflict with the terms of the mandate. Because the Union did not anticipate any immediate constitutional changes, the Permanent Mandates Commission did not enter upon a debate of this statement. It did state, however, that nothing expressed in these meetings should be interpreted as any sort of support for the "fifth province solution."[19]

For some time it seemed plausible that these statements might be the result of political maneuver and of the unfortunate choice of words rather than a conscious effort by the Union to secure maximum control over the area. However, since the demise of the League, there has been no doubt about the Union's position. The Union now maintains that it is sovereign over the area, using

16 Wright, *League Mandates*, 426-27.
17 Wright, *League Mandates*, 121.
18 Mandates Commission, 14th Sess., 12th meeting.
19 See *ibid.*, 27th Sess., 17 meeting and 31st Sess., 15th meeting.

statements made during the League period to support this sovereignty.

In 1945, Prime Minister Smuts once again tried to secure international recognition of annexation by asking the San Francisco Conference to terminate the South West Africa mandate and to recognize the incorporation of the territory. The conference, and the United Nations established by this conference, refused. The Union government retaliated by refusing to place the territory under the United Nations Trusteeship System and by not recognizing the jurisdiction of the United Nations over the area.

On May 7, 1945, the Union delegation to the San Francisco Conference stated its arguments for incorporation. At the time of the disposal of enemy territories under the Treaty of Versailles, the Union had questioned suitability of the mandatory form of administration and legislation over the area as an integral part of the Union. For twenty-five years the Union had administered the territory and had promoted to the utmost the well-being and social progress of the inhabitants. The Union had introduced a progressive policy of native administration, including local government through native councils, giving the natives a voice in the management of their own affairs. "In view of the contiguity and similarity in composition of the Native Peoples of South West Africa the Native Policy followed in South West Africa must always be aligned with that of the Union" because of the geographic, economic, and ethnologic relationship of the areas, the Union representative saw no prospect that the territory would ever exist as a separate state.[20] Prime Minister Smuts repeated these arguments before Committee Four of the General Assembly on November 4, 1946, saying both the Europeans and the non-Europeans of South West Africa wanted to become a part of Union territory. A vote taken in the mandate by the Union government showed that 208,850 persons were in favor of incorporation, while 33,520 were opposed. Out of the total population,

[20] United Nations, Fourth Committee Records, 1st Sess., 2nd Part (A/123, 1946), 200-201.

56,590 could not be consulted.[21] With the delegates of India and Russia leading the debate the validity of this vote was challenged immediately. It was later reported by the *Cape Times* that the government and its supporters agreed that tribal customs must be respected and that the decision of each chief obligated the entire tribe.[22] The Indian delegate, Sir Maharaj Singh, thought it would be odd if the South West African tribes wished to be incorporated in the Union of South Africa where Africans, Asiatics, and the members of the colored communities suffered from discrimination.[23] Committee Four rejected incorporation and recommended that the government of South Africa submit a trust agreement.

In March, 1947, Eric H. Louw of the opposition party, later to become minister of external affairs in the Nationalist government, introduced a motion in the Union House of Assembly calling for the incorporation of South West Africa. Louw said the Union Parliament should ignore the opinions of the United Nations on this question, saying that even the unprejudiced members of the U.N. were so confused that they concluded the information submitted did not warrant the group's approval of incorporation.

According to Louw, the Union's case should have been based on legal arguments. The Supreme Command and Allied Powers had assigned the territory to be administered as an integral part of the Union. The South African Railways Administration had been granted "full dominion" over the rail property of South West Africa, and there was also a treaty with Portugal which made reference to Union sovereignty over South West Africa. Louw also referred to the opinion in *Rex. v. Christian*, which said that sovereignty resided in the Union. A member of the House reminded Louw that he was quoting from a minority opinion. He replied that he was not, but even if he were, it would not matter as other judges had said the same thing in different words. Louw also did not mention that the League had objected to all these references to sovereignty.

21 Fourth Committee Records, 1st Sess., 2nd Part (Nov. 4, 1946), 62-65.
22 *New York Times*, Nov. 4, 1946, p. 16.
23 Fourth Committee Records, 1st Sess., 2nd Part (Nov. 27, 1946), 47-49.

Louw extended his legal debate by saying that while the League was in existence, the Union of South Africa acquired *de facto* possession over South West Africa and could have incorporated the territory at any time. With the passing of the League, South Africa acquired *de jure* possession of the territory.[24] Smuts objected to this reference to *de facto* and *de jure* possession because he felt it was a technical question and should not be raised. Smuts and a majority of the Union Parliament felt it unwise to make South West Africa a province of the Union at this time. Smuts felt that it would be better to continue cooperating with the United Nations by ruling the territory under the terms of the mandate.[25] In 1949, after the Nationalists had replaced the government of Smuts, Louw's incorporation bill was passed and, in essence, South West Africa became a fifth province of the Union. Daniel F. Malan, the new prime minister, stated that South West Africa was not an independent state and that it could not secede from the Union.[26] T. E. Dönges of the House of Assembly emphasized that the South West African Affairs Act of 1949 was not to be viewed as the final stage of incorporation. The act established an intermediate stage, but guaranteed the sovereignty of the Union in every respect.[27]

Union spokesmen generally maintained that the mandate for South West Africa expired with the League and that the United Nations is not the successor to the international rights and obligations of this body. They claim that the mandate constituted little less than annexation while the League existed and now sovereignty has passed to the Union. This interpretation has not been acceptable to the United Nations nor to the International Court of Justice. The United Nations is pledged to the doctrines of self-government, self-determination, and individual freedom and equality. Although South West Africa is an international mandate and the Union is not sovereign over the territory, the attitude of the United Nations might have been different if it had not been

---

[24] South Africa House of Assembly Debates, March 19, 1947, cols. 1319-46.
[25] South Africa House of Assembly Debates, March 19, 1947, cols. 1366-72.
[26] South Africa House of Assembly Debates, Feb. 21, 1949, col. 1640.
[27] South Africa House of Assembly Debates, Feb. 21, 1949, cols. 1479-81.

for the policy of apartheid. If the natives had political and economic rights, or perhaps if there were even a prospect that they eventually have these rights, conditions might well have been different. If South West Africa were truly self-governing, as the Union sometimes says it is, the mandate would automatically be terminated. The territory could then vote to make itself a part of the Union, and the United Nations could not object. The U.N. remains unconvinced that the Union government can be trusted with native development without international supervision. It is in this sense that apartheid is the root of all debate, posing a dilemma for all concerned. The United Nations cannot accept apartheid in the territory; South Africa cannot accept the territory without apartheid, because natives with equal rights and opportunities in a bordering territory would threaten apartheid at home.

FOUR:

THE QUESTION OF JURISDICTION

From the beginning of the organization in 1946 the United Nations has been faced with the tangled problem of jurisdiction over South West Africa. After unproductive efforts to find a solution through several councils and special committees, their work always complicated by lack of cooperation from the Union of South Africa, the U.N. submitted the dispute to the International Court of Justice in 1950 for an advisory opinion. The court, a U.N. branch, is composed of a panel of judges from disinterested nations elected for nine-year terms, and, if the parties to the dispute request it, two *ad hoc* judges, one selected by each party. Rather than offering a solution, however, the court's decision created a legal stalemate. The panel ruled that the Union of South Africa was not obliged to submit a trust agreement for the mandate. At the same time, though, the court recognized the U.N.'s right to supervise the administration of the territory and decided the mandate was still in effect.

In the dispute that followed, Union representatives pointed to the court's statement that they were not required to submit a trust agreement. The U.N. noted that the mandate was still existent and argued that the U.N. as supervisor could require a trust agreement.

This legal stalemate relates directly to the provision in the U.N. charter, which some critics have called a "gap."[1] According to the wording of the charter, submission of a trust agreement for areas under mandate is voluntary, although it seemed that during the various conferences forming the United Nations the delegates considered it to be obligatory. Only the Union of South Africa has taken advantage of this wording and has refused to submit a trust agreement.

A trusteeship system was first discussed in February, 1945, at the Yalta Conference, a meeting of nations who would hold permanent seats on the U.N. Security Council. The Dumbarton Oaks Proposals of 1944, which first outlined the United Nations and formed the basis for the San Francisco Conference in April, 1945, did not mention a trusteeship system. During the Yalta discussions the Soviet Union, the United States, and the United Kingdom agreed that the trusteeship system should be applied (1) to existing mandates under the League, (2) to territories detached from the enemy as a result of war, and (3) to other territories placed under the system voluntarily. Specific territories were mentioned neither at this conference nor at any of the subsequent formative conferences.

At the San Francisco conference, which drew up the United Nations charter, development of a trusteeship system was assigned to Committee Four (trusteeship) under Commission II (General Assembly). This committee was charged with outlining principles and mechanisms of a trusteeship system and presenting a draft to Commission II and Commission III (Security Council).

At a meeting of Committee Four the Egyptian delegation proposed a statement which would have required the Union of South Africa to submit a trust agreement: "The Trusteeship System shall apply to all territories now held under mandate."[2] However, the statement which was adopted as article 77 of the final U.N. charter read: "The trusteeship system shall apply to such territories in the following categories as may be placed thereunder by means of trusteeship agreements—territories now held under mandate; territories which may be detached from enemy states as a result of the Second World War; and territories voluntarily placed under the system by states responsible for their administration. It will be a matter for subsequent agreement as to which territories in

---

[1] Edwards Charmian Toussaint, *The Trusteeship System of the United Nations* (New York: Frederick A. Praeger, 1956), p. 46.

[2] *Documents of the United Nations Conference on International Organization* 16 vols. (San Francisco 1945), 468-69.

the foregoing categories will be brought under the trusteeship system and upon what terms." Article 79 stated that the terms of trusteeship, including the provision that any alteration or amendment, shall be agreed upon by the states directly concerned, including the mandatory power in the case of territories held under mandate by a member of the United Nations, and shall be approved as provided for in articles 83 and 85.

Paragraph 1 of article 80 provided that until such trust agreements had been concluded, nothing in the charter should be construed in or of itself to alter in any manner the rights whatsoever of any states or any peoples or the terms of existing international instruments to which members of the United Nations may respectively be parties. However, paragraph 1 should not be interpreted as grounds for delay or postponement of the negotiation and conclusion of agreements for placing mandated or other territories under the trusteeship system.[3]

The Union delegation came to San Francisco seeking recognition for the annexation of South West Africa, but they apparently were willing to accept a trust agreement, for the Union delegates seemed to be promoting a trusteeship system which would be acceptable to their government. A Union delegate told Committee Four that the open-door policy had not previously been applied in C mandates and that its application to their mandated area might be detrimental to the natives and was unacceptable to his government, though he did not demonstrate how this would be detrimental to the natives. In opposition to a Chinese proposal which envisaged direct international administration of trust territories, the Union representative reminded the committee that the terms of existing mandate agreements could not be altered without the consent of the mandatory.[4]

Committee Four noted that the title of a mandated area did not belong to the mandatory power, as it was the responsibility of

[3] *Charter of the United Nations*, ch. VII, arts. 77, 79, and 80.
[4] *International Organization Documents*, X, 434-39.

the League itself to pass title.[5] On April 18, 1946, when the League members voted the organization out of existence, no specific recommendations concerning the transfer of mandates to the United Nations were made. The League resolution stated that the assembly "recognizes that on the termination of the League's existence, its functions with respect to the mandated territories will come to an end, but notes that Chapters XI, XII and XIII of the Charter of the United Nations embody principles corresponding to those declared in Article 22 of the Covenant of the League." The assembly also "takes note of the expressed intentions of the Members of the League now administering territories under mandate to continue to administer them for the well-being and development of the peoples concerned in accordance with the obligations contained in the respective mandates, until other arrangements have been agreed between the United Nations and the respective mandatory powers."[6]

At the same meeting Leif Egeland, a representative of the Union, reminded the League that among the League's services necessarily left in abeyance at the outbreak of the Second World War and since suspended was its overseeing of the mandates. The Permanent Mandates Commission had had no sessions between 1939 and 1946, and Egeland said that since that last meeting new circumstances had arisen which obligated the mandatory powers to review the existing arrangements for administering their mandates. The Union government intended, he said, to formulate its case for South West Africa as an integral part of the Union at a forthcoming United Nations session. In the meantime the Union promised to continue administering the territory according to the obligations of the mandate until other arrangements could be agreed upon about the future status of the territory.[7] Union officials must have soon regretted this pledge, for when the United Nations refused to approve incorporation of South West Africa,

---

[5] *International Organization Documents*, 469.
[6] League of Nations, Plenary Debates, 21st Sess., 7th meeting.
[7] League of Nations, Plenary Debates, 21st Sess., 7th meeting.

the Union reversed its legal arguments, saying the obligations of the mandate died with the League. This reversal cast doubt upon the validity of this argument and the sincerity of Union officials in believing that sovereignty over South West Africa had passed to them.

The League transferred its documents and its technical and nonpolitical functions to the United Nations, but the rights and obligations concerning the mandates were not specifically transferred. The United Nations General Assembly promised to examine, or to submit to the appropriate organ of the United Nations, any request from members that the United Nations should assume functions or powers entrusted to the League by international instruments having a political character.[8] When the Union of South Africa asked the United Nations to approve the incorporation of their mandate, the South West Africa issue was placed on the General Assembly's agenda.

Much of the problem of jurisdiction of South West Africa stems from the League's failure to establish sovereignty over the mandates. One theory held that sovereignty was ascribed to the mandatory acting with the consent of the League. Quincy Wright, a scholar of international law, adopted this interpretation and argued that if a mandatory failed to carry out its obligations, the League Council could transfer the mandate. [9] Col. E. M. House, President Wilson's personal adviser, supported this view and thought the League must reserve the right to cancel a mandate in cases of mismanagement.[10] Another theory was that sovereignty was held in abeyance pending independence of the mandated peoples. There is no statement in the documents of the Paris Peace Conference, the records of the League, or in the mandate agreements which indicates that sovereignty was assigned to either

[8] Quincy Wright, *Mandates Under the League of Nations* (Chicago: University of Chicago Press, 1930), Wright 698-703.

[9] United Nations, General Assembly *Journal*, 1st Sess. (Feb. 12, 1946), 706-709.

[10] *The Intimate Papers of Colonel House*, ed. Charles Seymour (New York: Houghton Mifflin, 1928), IV, 294.

the League or to the administering powers. When the League ceased to exist, its members did not declare the mandate agreement null and void; on the contrary, they recognized that the administering powers should continue to rule their mandates according to these obligations until other arrangements could be made. In practice, the League had terminated a mandate under two conditions only—the presumption that a territory could govern itself or the termination of a mandate with the provision of certain guarantees. Iraq, the only case in the second category, received its independence and became a member of the League. The guarantee was a treaty between the administrator and the mandated area.

Another author, Hans Kelsen, argued that the mandate agreements ceased to be valid with the dissolution of the League. While the mandatories were not sovereign, they were the only powers in a position to extend sovereignty over the mandated areas. Should this be the case, only the section of the United Nations charter dealing with territories which were not self-governing (Chapter XI) would be applicable to a former mandate not placed under trusteeship.[11] In 1947 Prime Minister Smuts supported this interpretation, but he soon learned that it would be difficult to convince General Assembly members that South West Africa was a Union colony. The General Assembly challenged the Union's right to continue its administration, if it were to accept South Africa's argument that South West Africa no longer was a mandate.

Had the United Nations charter been specific in placing all mandates under trusteeship and had it named particular territories, the legal debate about sovereignty and jurisdiction would not have developed. It is unlikely, however, that all parties would have agreed that their territories automatically fall under the system, and this would have jeopardized the creation of a workable trustee organization. For example, the United States was not in a position

[11] *The Law of the United Nations* (London: Stevens and Sons, LTD., 1950), 598-603.

to press for specific agreement concerning South West Africa when it was undetermined about what the U.S. would do with the Pacific island mandate taken from the Japanese. (Eventually, the mandate was placed under the trusteeship system as a strategic trust, which gave the United States virtual veto power over policy concerning the area.)

Aside from the legalistic debate there is a strategic point to be considered. Though the Union denies obligation to submit a trust agreement to the United Nations and though it believes League rights over the mandate have not descended to the United Nations, South Africa accepted the competence of the U.N. to terminate the mandate agreement. It requested permission to annex South West Africa from the United Nations, not Allied Powers, who had assigned the mandate, or any other group. This action led to the suggestion that if the U.N. had the authority to terminate the mandate, it also would have the authority to suggest an alternative solution. Only after the U.N. refused to grant the Union's request did that government challenge the authority of the United Nations to determine the jurisdiction of South West Africa.

Most member nations thought the United Nations had strong moral justification for its actions and felt the U.N. was observing the spirit of the organization's charter. No mandatory other than the Union of South Africa had raised the question of legal obligations; other mandatories felt that it was in their interest and in the interests of the mandated peoples to submit trust agreements to the United Nations. A. T. Wanless, a member of the Union House, said the U.N. was justified in assuming the rights which it had assumed, even though they had not been transferred to it specifically, on a moral basis. He said these rights had been assumed by general and common consent throughout the world, and it was too late for the Union to claim, because of expedience, that the United Nations was not the logical inheritor of the rights, obligations, and duties of the League.

In evaluating the Union's actions one must not overlook the

attitude of Prime Minister Smuts. He had participated in the creation of both the League of Nations and the United Nations. Although he wanted control of South West Africa, he had an international outlook and guarded the Union's international position. Also, he perhaps did not anticipate the violent objections which were to be raised in opposition to the Union's incorporation of South West Africa.

In 1948 the government of Smuts was replaced by the Nationalist party under Prime Minister Daniel F. Malan. It is doubtful that Union actions would have differed greatly had Smuts remained in power, but Smut did withdraw his plan to incorporate South West Africa after the United Nations refused to give its approval. Smuts had promised to continue the administration of South West Africa in the spirit of the mandate and to submit reports concerning conditions within the mandate to the United Nations. The Nationalist government stated in 1949 that the mandate had ended with the dissolution of the League and served notice that it no longer would submit reports to the United Nations. Smuts might have been forced to make these same decisions, as discussions in the U.N. based upon the report submitted by the Union were critical of the Union's policy. By this time all other former mandates either had been granted independence or had been placed under the trusteeship system. A February 9, 1946, plenary meeting of the General Assembly had urged that trust agreements be submitted not later than the second part of the first session.[13] All mandatories except the Union of South Africa complied. The General Assembly passed a number of resolution strongly urging submission of a trust agreement for South West Africa and, when these brought no results, submitted the case to the International Court of Justice.

On December 6, 1949, the General Assembly posed the following questions to the court: Does the Union of South Africa con-

[12] Union of South Africa, House of Assembly Debates, April 11, 1947, cols. 2581-83.
[13] United Nations, General Assembly Resolutions, 1st Sess., Res. 11(I).

tinue to have international obligations under the mandate of South West Africa and, if so, what are these obligations? Secondly, are the provisions of chapter XII of the charter applicable to the territory? Finally has the Union of South Africa the competence to modify the international status of South West Africa, and, if not, where does this competence rest?[14]

On July 11, 1950, the court, composed of Judges Basdevant of France, Guerrero of El Salvador, Alvarez of Chile, Hackworth of the United States, Winiarski of Poland, Zoricic of Yugoslavia, De Visscher of Belgium, Sir Arnold McNair of the United Kingdom, Klaestad of Norway, Badawi Pasha of Egypt, Krylov of the U.S.S.R., Read of Canada, Hsu Mo of China, and Azevedo of Brazil handed down its advisory opinion. The court held unanimously that South West Africa was a territory under the international mandate assumed on December 17, 1920. The panel reasoned that South West Africa was still a territory under international mandate, because the international rules governing the mandate constituted an international status for the territory, recognized by all the League members, including the Union of South Africa. The creation of the mandatory system did not involve any cession of territory or transfer of sovereignty to the Union of South Africa, the court held.

Because supervision resided with the League Council, the functions exercised by the Union under the mandate were international in character, the court decided. The Union was obligated to report to this body and to submit disputes related to the mandate agreement to the jurisdiction of the Permanent Court of International Justice if any member of the League requested this. Furthermore, the authority which the Union exercised over South West Africa was based on the mandate; if the mandate had lapsed, as the Union had contended, the Union's authority over South West Africa equally would have lapsed. The rights derived from the mandate could not be retained without the obligations, and

[14] General Assembly Resolutions, 4th Sess., Res. 338 (IV).

it obviously was intended that the rights of states and of peoples be safeguarded under all circumstances and in all respects until each territory should be placed under the trusteeship system.[15]

The court decided unanimously that the provisions of chapter XII of the charter were applicable to South West Africa because they provided a means by which the territory might be brought under the trusteeship system. By a vote of eight to six, the court advised that the provisions of chapter XII of the charter do not impose a legal obligation upon the Union to place the territory under trusteeship and rejected the contention that paragraph 2 of article 80 required this. The judges ruled that the trusteeship system was not created for mandated territories only and these territories were not automatically placed under trusteeship, because an agreement implies consent of the parties concerned. Furthermore, the obligation to negotiate does not assure the conclusion of an agreement, the majority advised. However, the court noted that the normal way of modifying the international status of South West Africa would be to place it under the trusteeship system.[16]

Dissenting opinions on this point were given by Judges Alvarez, De Visscher, Krylov, Guerrero, Zoricic, and Badawi Pasha. These judges believed that the Union was obligated to enter into negotiations with a view to concluding a trust agreement and that this obligation extended beyond negotiation.[17]

The court voted twelve to two that the Union of South Africa's international obligations stated in article 22 of the Covenant of the League of Nations and in the mandate agreement were still in effect. In addition, the court said the Union was obligated to transmit petitions from the inhabitants of the territory. Since the United Nations was to exercise the supervisory function, petitions and annual reports were to be submitted to this body. The court also held that the United Nations was the successor to the rights and obligations of the League and that the International Court of

[15] International Court of Justice, *Reports of Judgments, Advisory Opinions and Orders* (The Hague: 1950), 132-33.

[16] *International Court Reports,* 139-41.

[17] *International Court Reports,* 174-92.

Justice was the successor to the Permanent Court of International Justice.[18]

The court's decision that South West Africa possessed an international status virtually assured the ruling that the obligations of the Union under the League mandate continued. In reasoning that the Union's obligations outlived the League, the judges pointed to article 80, paragraph one of the charter, which safeguards the rights of states and of peoples of mandated areas pending the conclusion of trusteeship agreements. The court ruled that international supervision and the requirement that a mandatory submit periodic reports to a supervisory organization are necessary for this protection. Under article 10, the judges decided the General Assembly is competent to receive and examine these reports and to make recommendations to a mandatory.

More debatable from a legal point-of-view is the court's decision that the United Nations is the successor to the rights and obligations of the League of Nations. By political and moral considerations this should have been the case, but the legal argument on this point is weak. Supervision is necessary, however, and the United Nations is the logical group to perform this function.

The supervision of the mandate by the United Nations should conform as far as possible to the procedures followed by the League Council, the court advised, and the degree of supervision exercised by the General Assembly should not exceed that applied under the mandate agreement. Although the right of the native inhabitants of a mandate to petition the supervising agent was not contained in article 22 of the League Covenant or in the mandate agreement, the League adopted this right into its rules on January 31, 1923. This right was maintained by article 80, paragraph 1 of the United Nations charter.

Actions by the Union government supported the court's conclusion, the panel of judges ruled. In the 1946 League resolution disbanding that organization the League members ended their functions relative to the mandated territories with the understand-

[18] *International Court Reports*, 143.

ing that the mandates were to continue until other arrangements had been made. The Union government stated that its obligations continued, and it acted accordingly.[19]

The court agreed unanimously that the Union of South Africa acting alone could not modify the international status of South West Africa, and the competence to determine and to modify the status of the territory rested with the Union acting with the consent of the United Nations. Article 7 of the mandate agreement provided that the consent of the League Council was required for the modification of the terms of the mandate, and the United Nations charter granted the General Assembly the authority to approve alterations or amendments of trust agreements. The court felt, by analogy, it could be inferred that the same procedure was applicable to any modification of status in a territory not placed under the Trusteeship Council. The actions of the Union government indicated an acceptance of this interpretation. The Union of South Africa requested that the General Assembly approve modification of the status of South West Africa, and this act constituted a recognition of the competence of the General Assembly in this matter, the court concluded.

The reception of the court's opinion was varied. On December 13, 1950, the General Assembly accepted the decision by a vote of forty-five to six with five abstentions. The negative votes and the abstentions were caused by several factors. Several nations did not vote for this motion because they preferred one submitted by Committee Four which listed the findings of the court in their entirety and set a specific deadline for the completion of negotiations with the Union government. Also, the nations disagreed as to how the court's opinion could best be implemented. These were the chief reasons for the abstentions of Australia, Belgium, Bolivia, Colombia, and New Zealand. The negative votes were cast by the Union of Soviet Socialist Republics, Byelorussia, Czechoslovakia, Poland, and the Ukraine.[20] The fact that several

[19] *International Court Reports*, 134-38.
[20] General Assembly, Plenary Meetings, 5th Sess., Vol. I (Dec. 13, 1950), 627-32.

of the Communist countries voted with Union did not imply a common appraisal of the court's opinion. The Russians maintained that the Union was obligated either to submit South West Africa to trusteeship or to grant its independence. Instead of accepting the court's opinion, the Russians introduced a motion of censure against the Union of South Africa. Some of the Communist nations, in an effort to influence favorably the Afro-Asian bloc of the United Nations, assumed leadership of the opposition to South African policies.

Curiously, although the Union rejected the opinion, it was used by that government as a legal defense for its refusal to submit a trust agreement. Because the court agreed that there was no binding obligation to place South West Africa under trusteeship, the 1950 advisory opinion constituted a partial victory for the Union of South Africa. The Union government, however, re-fused to accept as binding portions of the opinion which said that South West Africa was an international territory and that the Union was obligated to submit reports and petitions to the United Nations.

The court's opinion was significant for the United Nations be-cause it constituted a legal sanction for many of the actions already taken by that body and justified actions which would be taken in the future. After receiving the court's opinion, the General Assembly established a special committee which was authorized to conduct negotiations with the Union and to examine reports, petitions, and other materials relating to South West Africa re-ceived by the Secretary-General of the United Nations.[21] The 1950 opinion established the United Nation's right to supervise admin-istration of the mandate, and because it recognized the Interna-tional Court of Justice as the successor of the Permanent Interna-tional Court of Justice, it paved the way for the contentious proceedings brought by Ethiopia and Liberia in 1960.

The opinion opened the door for new negotiations between the United Nations and the Union of South Africa, but these negotia-

[21] General Assembly Resolutions, 5th Sess., Supp. No. 20, Res. 449A(V).

tions ended in stalemate. Relations between the Union and the United Nations from the end of the Second World War until the 1950 advisory opinion were characterized by uncertainty on the part of all parties concerned, as each member nation was trying to determine what its position on the South West Africa issue should be and how this position could be justified legally. This period marked the high point of Union cooperation with the United Nations.

The court's opinion removed a degree of uncertainty, but it did not resolve the conflict which existed. It merely made the parties more vehement in many of their original arguments—the General Assembly continuing to believe the Union should submit a trust agreement, while the Union, backed in part by the court, continuing to refuse. Supported by the opinion, the United Nations intensified its supervisory effort, and the Union retaliated by withdrawing the little cooperation it had extended. The many attempts at compromise on the South West Africa issue all have failed on one point: the Union government will not accept United Nations supervision over its administration of the mandated area and the United Nations will not agree to less.

FIVE:

METHODS OF SUPERVISION

Although the 1950 opinion of the International Court of Justice clearly gave to the United Nations power to oversee the Union's administration of South West Africa, the court did not specify the manor of supervision, other than imposing the limitation that U.N. supervision should not exceed that which was authorized under the League of Nations. The court ruled that the U.N. had a right to expect reports and petitions from the Union administration, but the critical reception of the 1946 report which the Union submitted made that government unwilling to continue reporting. Also, the voting procedures of the United Nations and the League of Nations differed, and the court's opinion had not made clear which set of rules should be applied to issues relating to South West Africa. Before these questions were resolved, the ingenuity of the General Assembly was tested severely, and the International Court was consulted twice more.

The controversy concerning the 1946 report began when Prime Minister Smuts, not admitting any responsibility for submitting reports but anxious to curry favor for his proposal to annex South West Africa, agreed to send to the United Nations annual reports on the mandate for purposes of information. He felt this would demonstrate the good faith of his government.

Presentation of this first report posed something of a dilemma for Prime Minister Smuts and other Union officials. Since they did not regard South West Africa as a trust and since they did not want to recognize United Nations' authority, they did not want to submit the report to the Trusteeship Council. Smuts proposed submitting the report under chapter XI, article 73(e) of the charter, the provision covering non-self-governing territories.[1] This article provides for submission of technical information to the

Secretary-General. Since the Union had neither annexed South West Africa nor placed it under the trusteeship system, South Africa presumed it had the same responsibilities which all United Nations members had regarding non-self-governing territories. The Union argued that since the League had been dispersed, the obligation to submit petitions no longer could be exercised, because that obligation presupposed a jurisdiction which would exist only in conjunction with a right to control and to supervise. This right was not held by the U.N., the Union claimed.[2] The chief disadvantage of submitting the report under chapter XI was that the information could be debated by the General Assembly.

Prime Minister Smuts had promised to report under the terms of the mandate, but nothing was said about reporting under chapter VI. Eric Louw, a Union House of Assembly delegate and a member of the opposition party, was vehement in his criticism of Smuts on this point. Louw thought the Union would be as vulnerable in submitting the report under chapter XI as it would be in submitting it to the Trusteeship Council. The wording of chapter XI, similar to the rule governing A mandates, required that the mandatory take steps to secure self-government within the territory. Louw asked Smuts if he were prepared to tell the House of Assembly that he intended to promote political advancement for the native population of South West Africa.[3] Actually, Smuts had intended to maintain the spirit, but not the letter, of the law in submitting the voluntary reports.

The United Nations General Assembly ignored completely the terms under which the Union had submitted the 1946 report, however, and authorized the Trusteeship Council to examine the report and to submit its observations to the General Assembly. There was considerable debate upon the legality of this action. Certainly, the Union had no legal justification for saying that

[1] United Nations, Fourth Committee Records, Ch. V, 2nd Sess. (Sept. 27, 1947), 15-16.

[2] Ibid., 16.

[3] Union of South Africa, House of Assembly Debates, March 19, 1947, cols. 1335-46.

South West Africa was a colony and that the Union would, therefore, report to the United Nations under the provisions of chapter XI of the charter. The General Assembly, on the other hand, had no real legal right to treat the report as a one from a trust territory. Article 87(a) of the charter authorizes the Trusteeship Council to examine reports from trust areas only. Finally, the council decided that special factors must be kept in mind since the area was not under trusteeship, but that it would examine the report in the same way as it would a report from a trust area.[4]

It would have been more legally correct if the General Assembly had established a special committee to examine the Union's 1946 report. The jurisdiction which the United Nations exercised derived from the obligations under the mandate and from the fact that the Union had submitted the report. While the General Assembly was in no way bound to accept the arguments of the Union claiming the non-self-governing status for South West Africa, it might have been wiser for the United Nations to have modeled its procedures after those used by the League. Nevertheless, it is doubtful, that the Union's attitude would have differed had the United Nations established an *ad hoc* committee replicating the Permanent Mandates Commission. No matter what the composition of a United Nations body, its decisions would have been essentially the same.

On December 1, 1947, the Trusteeship Council decided that the Union should be notified of the time the South West Africa report would be examined and advised that they could send a representative if they wished. The Union declined. While the council was attempting to decide just what procedures it should follow in this case, the Belgian member asked whether the council could admit parties other than the government representative. He thought not, for article 80 of the charter stated that until a trust agreement has been reached, nothing shall alter the rights of any state or of any people. Admitting the testimony of anyone other than the

[4] United Nations, Trusteeship Council, *Official Records*, 2nd Sess., 1st Part (Dec. 1, 1947) 120-32.

Union's official representative would be contrary to the usual practice of the Permanent Mandates Commission.[5] The president of the Trusteeship Council ruled that sources of information other than the Union's report could be considered, but several members objected to this ruling.[6]

The council decided the report on South West Africa did not contain sufficient information, and the members formulated a list of fifty questions for the Union government. The Union government answered the questions, but stated once again that it was under no obligation to do so.[7] Fearing that such action by the council might imply acceptance of the South West Africa situation, the Russian council member said that since the legal status of South West Africa was undetermined, the council should not consider the reply to the questionnaire.[8]

The findings of the Trusteeship Council, submitted to the General Assembly on August 4, 1948, constituted an indictment against South African policies in South West Africa. The council was concerned that the indigenous inhabitants of the territory had no representation in the governing bodies or in the administration. Also, council members deplored the system of reserves and urban segregation and expressed concern because the traditional lands of the natives had not been restored. The council considered that the expenditure of little more than 10 percent of the budget on the indigenous population was neither equitable nor adequate. The body was concerned about the low level of native wages, the use of prison labor, and the disparity between the educational facilities provided for the European children and those provided for the natives.[9] All the criticisms by the Trusteeship Council concerned native policies, and all these conditions are a part of and a reflection of apartheid.

[5] *Ibid.*, 125-32.
[6] *Ibid.*, 472-509.
[7] United Nations, Trusteeship Records, 3rd Sess., Supp. (T/175, Dec., 1948), 51-52.
[8] Trusteeship Records, 3rd Sess., 406-10.
[9] Trusteeship Records, 3rd Sess., Supp., 223-30.

When, following Smuts' loss of power, the Union announced it would submit no additional reports to the United Nations, the Trusteeship Council said it could no longer exercise a supervisory function.[10] The Union delegate gave four reasons for the decision to stop reporting to the United Nations. First, there appeared to be little understanding within the United Nations of the unique relationship between South West Africa and the Union. Second, it appeared the U.N. gave little recognition to the Union's assurances that the territory would continue to be administered in the spirit of the mandate. Third, the information which had been furnished voluntarily was being used to criticize in an unwarranted manner and to censure the South African government. Finally, the Union did not agree that its submission of reports indicated its accountability to the United Nations for its administration of South West Africa.[11] The Union's position left several important questions unanswered. What was this unique relationship between South West Africa and the Union? Did the mandate agreement state that South West Africa was a territory where the Union could apply policies which were detrimental to the well-being of the natives? Why would the United Nations recognize the assurances of the Union concerning the mandate when Union conduct did not warrant this recognition? The submission of reports to the United Nations did constitute a recognition of the jurisdiction of that body in the South West Africa case. Did the Union authorities think that jurisdiction would cease if reports no longer were submitted?

Louw, while he was still a member of the opposition, gave a more accurate picture of the Union's motivations. Louw felt that the Union could not afford to submit another report because of the repercussions United Nations discussions had on native opinion in South West Africa and the Union. The submission of reports amounted to placing the issue on the agenda of the General Assembly. If the United Nations had any excuse for intervention

[10] Trusteeship Records, 5th Sess., Supp. No. 1 (July 20, 1949), 191.
[11] Fourth Committee Records, 4th Sess. (July 11, 1949), 44.

in the administration of South West Africa, it would use its authority to apply a bill of human rights in the area.[12] The refusal to report to the United Nations can be blamed on the Nationalist party which came to power in 1949, but it is possible that Prime Minister Smuts might have been forced into the same decision.

The refusal of the Union government to supply the United Nations with further information on South West Africa created a problem for the General Assembly. When the 1950 advisory opinion confirmed the General Assembly's contention that the Union was obligated to submit reports and petitions, U.N. members hoped Union officials would reverse their decision. To facilitate cooperation between the Union and the United Nations and to implement the 1950 decision, the General Assembly established an *ad hoc* committee which was to supervise South West African administration in accordance with procedures used by the Permanent Mandates Commission. The committee—composed of representatives of Syria, Thailand, the United Kingdom, the United States, and Uruguay—was authorized to conduct negotiations with the Union government and to examine reports, petitions, and other materials relating to the territory which might be transmitted to the Secretary-General. Some members of the General Assembly felt that the Union might submit to United Nations supervision if that organization agreed to the procedures of the League.[13] Conditions were not the same, however; this was not the League of Nations, but the United Nations; the year was not 1920, but 1950. Though the U.N. might follow the procedures of the League, its members would not share the views on colonial and racial policy League members had held. The General Assembly's refusal to approve incorporation and its handling of the 1946 report had made Union officials painfully aware of this change in attitude.

The Union of South Africa did agree to negotiate with the *ad hoc* committee, but it did not transmit petitions and reports, so the

[12] South Africa House of Assembly Debates, March 19, 1947, cols. 135-46.
[13] United Nations, General Assembly Resolutions, 5th Sess., Supp. No. 20, Res. 449A(V).

committee found it impossible to exercise effective supervision over the mandate. In an attempt to remedy this situation the General Assembly established in 1953 a larger committee with more extensive powers—the Committee on South West Africa—composed of delegates from Brazil, Mexico, Norway, Pakistan, Syria, Thailand, and Uruguay. This committee was asked to establish supervision and to formulate a procedure for examining reports and petitions which would conform, as far as possible, to procedures followed by the Permanent Mandates Commission.[14]

The 1950 advisory opinion had left several questions unanswered, and the actions of the Union government had raised additional ones. How could the United Nations establish effective supervision if the Union did not transmit reports and petitions? Could a committee of the United Nations formulate its own report? Did the General Assembly have the legal authority to continue to hear oral petitions from individuals who were qualified to speak on South West Africa? In voting on important issues should the United Nations follow the principle of unanimity used by the League, or should it follow the provisions of its own charter which stated that important questions could be decided by a two-thirds majority? If it followed the principle of unanimity, would it be violating the provision of its own charter? Also, if a unanimous vote were required, would not the Union of South Africa have an absolute veto over the decisions of the General Assembly?

The Committee on South West Africa proposed to the General Assembly the following solutions to these procedural questions. Special rule A provided that the General Assembly should receive an annual report on the administration of South West Africa from the committee. If the Union government refused to supply information, the committee was authorized to prepare its own report. The General Assembly was also to receive the observations of the committee, together with the comments of the Union representative, should South Africa choose to appoint one. The

[14] General Assembly Resolutions, 8th Sess., Res. 749A(VIII).

committee hoped that this procedure would establish effective supervision over the mandate, even if the Union continued refusing to cooperate. Special rule B stated that as a rule the General Assembly should be guided by the conclusions of the committee. This procedure would conform closely with that of the League. Special rule F provided that decisions of the General Assembly on questions relating to reports and petitions about South West Africa should be regarded as important questions within the meaning of article 18, paragraph 2, of the United Nations charter, meaning these decisions could be made only by a two-thirds majority vote. The Committee on South West Africa recommended that rule F be adopted by the General Assembly only with the concurring vote of the Union. Without the approval of the Union, the question should be sent to the International Court of Justice for an advisory opinion, the committee suggested.[15]

When these recommendations came to a vote on October 11, 1954, they were accepted by the General Assembly with thirty-three votes in favor, three against, and fifteen abstentions. Most of those who voted against these procedural rules felt that the International Court of Justice should be consulted first. The Union of South Africa voted against the committee's proposals because it did not recognize the right of United Nations supervision and because special rule F did not conform to the voting procedure of the League. A motion to submit special rule F to the court, however, failed by a vote of thirteen to eight, with twenty-nine abstentions.

Rule A, which stated that the Committee on South West Africa could prepare its own annual report if the Union government did not submit one, was a most significant step in the establishment of supervisory machinery by the United Nations. By the time the committee was established, a majority of the General Assembly concluded that they could expect no cooperation from the Union of South Africa and whatever supervision was provided

[15] United Nations, Report of the Committee on South West Africa, 9th Sess., Supp. No. 14 (A/2666, 1954), 13-14.

for administering South West Africa would have to be carried out despite the Union's objections. Rule A would permit the Committee on South West Africa to compile and to publicize all information available from sources other than the Union government. The committee could not function with maximum effectiveness under these circumstances, but there was no meaningful alternative.

The controversy over the legality of the voting procedure in special rule F continued, until a majority within the General Assembly was pressured into submitting the question to the International Court of Justice for an advisory opinion. Several delegations—including Norway, Thailand, and the United States—said that without a request from the General Assembly for an advisory opinion on voting procedure, their delegations would not consider a resolution based on reports provided by the Committee on South West Africa.[16] After the members of Committee Four again voted down a resolution to consult the court, the representatives of the United States, Iraq, and Sweden refused to serve further on the committee.[17] This refusal would have limited still further the possible effectiveness of this governing committee. Most U.N. members felt there was no reason to ask the court's opinion and that rule F was in keeping with the procedures established in the 1950 opinion. Moreover, the United Nations charter did not provide an alternative voting procedure. Other members felt it was necessary to do everything possible to secure the cooperation of the Union and thought if the United Nations were armed with an additional legal opinion, perhaps the Union government would alter its course.

The refusal by several delegations to serve on the Committee on South West Africa, however, reopened the debate within the General Assembly on the legality of rule F. This time the delegates voted to seek the court's opinion. Even though the issue was forced by a minority, the fact that the General Assembly was

[16] Fourth Committee Records, 9th Sess. (Oct. 19, 1954), 77-80.
[17] Fourth Committee Records, 191-96.

willing to turn to the court for a decision to end legal controversy and reestablish participation and cooperation of most members was an indication of its strength. While the General Assembly could not resolve the legal issue, the court could.

The South African delegate voted against the resolution to submit the question of voting procedure to the court, saying it was not necessary to seek another opinion. The court had said procedures should conform to those used by the League, and the court could not have been unaware of the voting procedure used by that body.[18] The Union delegate did not want another opinion, for as long as doubt remained, he could apply his own legal interpretation. If the Union government had been concerned seriously with legality, it would have accepted the 1950 opinion.

The court's opinion of June 7, 1955, concluded unanimously that special rule F was a correct interpretation of its advisory opinion of 1950. Four separate, but not dissenting, opinions were filed by Judges Basdevant of France, Klaestad of Norway, Kojevnikov of the U.S.S.R., and Lauterpacht of the United Kingdom. The majority opinion, approved by Judges Hackworth of the United States, Badawi Pasha of Egypt, Read of Canada, Guerrero of El Salvador, Winiarski of Poland, Zoricic of Yugoslavia, Hsu Mo of China, Armand-Ugon of Uruguay, Zafrullo Khan of Pakistan, Moreno Quintana of Argentina, and Cordova of Mexico.

These centered upon two arguments. The 1950 opinion did not state that the General Assembly must follow procedures identical to those used by the League in its supervision of the mandates. The same procedure used by the General Assembly to approve trusteeship agreements should be used to approve modifications of the international status of South West Africa, the court ruled.[19] This procedure calls for a two-thirds majority vote. The second argument of the court in defense of special rule F was that the

18 United Nations, General Assembly, Plenary Meetings, 9th Sess. (Nov. 23, 1954), 321-30.
19 International Court of Justice, *Reports of Judgments, Advisory Opinions and Orders* (The Hague: 1955), 55.

unanimity rule had not always been applied in the operation of the League. Any alteration in the terms of a mandate did require unanimity, but it was an established principle that no country was the judge of its own case. The court's judges doubted that mandatories holding a seat on the League Council would have been permitted to exercise a veto in a way which frustrated the operation of the mandate system. It was also the established practice of the League that an abstention did not constitute a negative vote, the court noted.[20]

In a separate statement Judge Basdevant said that special rule F was the correct voting procedure for the General Assembly, because that body could not alter the voting procedure set forth in article 18 of the U.N. charter. Judge Klaestad said the voting procedure was valid because the obligations of the Union under this system of supervision were no more onerous than those under the mandates system. Since a resolution passed by a two-thirds vote of the General Assembly without the concurring vote of the Union is not binding, their obligations had not increased. Judge Lauterpacht stated that he did not wish to base his conclusion upon the proposition that General Assembly resolutions had no binding effect at all, but they were of a legal potency lower than the resolutions of the League. In the fourth separate opinion Judge Kojevnikov said that while he voted with the court, he did not wish for this to imply his consent to the 1950 opinion. He felt that the provisions of chapter XII of the charter did impose a legal obligation upon the Union to place South West Africa under trusteeship.[21] While a two-thirds majority of the General Assembly accepted the 1955 opinion, the Union of South Africa did not.[22]

The only beneficial result of this advisory opinion was to reassure the members of the General Assembly that their voting procedures were legally correct. There was no reason to assume that the Union of South Africa would be bound by this opinion when its leaders had not accepted the 1950 opinion, which estab-

[20] *International Court Reports*, 40-60.
[21] *International Courts Reports*, 78-123.
[22] General Assembly Resolutions, 10th Sess., Supp. No. 19, Res. 934.

lished the right of the United Nations to supervise the administration of South West Africa.

More disturbing to the Union of South Africa than any other aspect of United Nations' supervision was the decision of Committee Four to accept oral petitions. The Union government maintained that after the demise of the League, it was no longer obligated to transmit written petitions. Even after the 1950 opinion of the International Court of Justice, which advised that this obligation remained, the Union government forwarded no petitions. The Permanent Mandates Commission accepted only those petitions which had been forwarded and commented upon by the mandatory power, but the United Nations was empowered to accept oral testimony as well as written petitions. Because the Union government had transmitted no petitions, a majority of Committee Four felt justified in accepting the oral opinions of persons who were qualified. Though this practice had the advantage of securing more information, it further alienated the Union.

The first oral petitioner to appear before Committee Four was the Reverend Michael Scott, who spoke on November 26, 1949, in behalf of the leaders of the Herero, the Ovambo, and the Bantu people. Union officials strongly opposed the hearing. The native leaders had wanted to appear before Committee Four in person, but Scott intimated that Union authorities had denied them passports. The Union delegate refused to sit with Committee Four during this hearing, lest his presence imply consent.[23]

From 1949 until 1955, when the General Assembly submitted the question of oral petitions to the court, the Union of South Africa protested the granting of these hearings. At the plenary meeting of the General Assembly on January 18, 1952, Mr. T. E. Dönges of the Union delivered a belligerent attack upon Committee Four. Dönges charged that the rights of the Union were being trampled underfoot. The Union had preferred to act upon principles calculated to uphold the sanctity of the charter, and

[23] Fourth Committee Records, 4th Sess. (Nov. 23, 1954), 213-19.

this had made the debate somewhat one-sided, he said. The Union had not defended itself against these misrepresentations, because this might be admitting the right of the United Nations to discuss, and thus to interfere, in matters of domestic jurisdiction. The Union of South Africa would then be a party to the violation of the charter, the representative claimed. The Union government hardly could argue that the South West Africa issue fell within its domestic jurisdiction, since the International Court had already decided the territory had an international status. Some of Dönges' legal arguments, however, had merit. He felt that Committee Four had acted beyond its legal competence in taking oral petitions from representatives of a country which was not a trust territory. The charter made no provision for the hearing of petitions except in the case of trust territories, and the League had not permitted oral petitions related to mandates. An *ad hoc* committee had already been established to receive petitions in accordance with the procedures of the League.[24] Dönges did not seem to feel that because the Union had not forwarded a single petition, the legal merit of this argument was weakened.

When the court delivered its third advisory opinion on June 1, 1956, it concluded by a vote of eight to five that it would not be inconsistent with its 1950 opinion for the General Assembly to authorize oral hearings before the Committee on South West Africa. The court placed two qualifications on the granting of oral petitions: (1) that petitioners heard orally must already have submitted written petitions, and (2) that the General Assembly must be satisfied that a hearing was necessary for maintaining effective international supervision of the administration of the mandate. The court explained that the 1950 opinion authorized the General Assembly to safeguard the sacred trust of civilization through effective international supervision, and the court did not intend to restrict the activity of the General Assembly to measures which actually had been used by the League.

The basis for the majority opinion was that the noncooperation

[24] General Assembly, Plenary Meetings, 6th Sess. (Jan. 18, 1952), 356-63.

of the Union had made the rules concerning petitions inoperative and had hindered the ability of the General Assembly to supervise effectively. Although the League had never heard oral petitions, it had been within the competence of the League to authorize them, the panel of judges ruled.[25] The League once had ruled against hearing oral petitions (in 1927), but the Permanent Mandates Commission report held that such exceptional measures would be acceptable if the information were not otherwise available.[26]

The court felt that oral hearings could not be presumed to add to the mandatory's burden. It was in the interest of the mandatory, as well as in the successful operation of the mandatory system, that the information submitted be as accurate as possible. Adhering to the majority opinion were Judges Hackworth, Winiarski, Klaestad, Read, Kojevnikov, Zafrulla Khan, Lauterpacht, and Cordova.

Judge Lauterpacht stated in a separate opinion that admission of oral hearings was not inconsistent with the 1950 ruling so long as the mandatory refused to cooperate, but if the mandatory complied with its obligation to send reports and to transmit petitions, the oral hearings no longer would be justified.[27] Judges Badawi, Basdevant, Hsu Mo, Armand-Ugon, and Moreno Quintana, in filing a dissenting opinion, concluded that since the League had not heard oral petitions, it would be inconsistent with the 1950 opinion for the United Nations to exceed the practice of the League. Such hearings might be justified on the basis of the noncooperation of the Union government, these judges wrote, but the General Assembly had not asked the court to consider that point.[28]

Once again the Union of South Africa refused to be bound by the court's opinion. Nonetheless, the decision was a victory for the United Nations. In the three advisory opinions the Inter-

[25] *International Court Reports*, 40-44.
[26] *International Court Reports*, 28.
[27] *International Court Reports*, 48.
[28] *International Court Reports*, 60-71.

national Court of Justice only once failed to give the General Assembly the legal backing it desired, the one exception being the opinion that the Union of South Africa was not obligated to submit a trust agreement.

Supported by these opinions, the General Assembly set up a workable system for supervising the administration of South West Africa. With legal justification for formulating its own annual reports and for hearing oral petitions, the United Nations was able to improve its supervision considerably. Each year the General Assembly heard an annual report—prepared alternately by the Committee on South West Africa, the Special Committee for South West Africa, or the Special Committee on Colonialism.[29]

A major drawback in the supervision by the U.N. was the Union's continued refusal to send a representative to hearings about South West Africa. Without hearing from a Union representative, the General Assembly had no way of checking the validity of its information about the Union's administration of the mandate.

Despite the roadblocks, the General Assembly accomplished two main purposes in its debates on South West Africa—helping to kindle revulsion of world opinion about South African policy and making the South West African native aware of his exploited position and of the possibility of change.

[29] General Assembly Resolution 749A of Nov. 28, 1953, created the Committee on South West Africa which was assigned the responsibility of supervising the administration of South West Africa and authorized to examine oral petitions and prepare an annual report for the General Assembly. On Dec. 19, 1961, by Resolution 1702, the General Assembly created a new and larger committee (the Special Committee for South West Africa) and assigned to it the functions previously exercised by the Committee on South West Africa. The Special Committee on the Situation with regard to the Implementation of the Declaration on the Granting of Independence of Colonial Countries and Peoples was established on Dec. 14, 1962, by Resolution 1805 and was assigned to supervise South West Africa administration.

SIX:

FAILURE OF COMPROMISE

Within the United Nations since 1946 two approaches toward solution of the South West Africa problem have been dominant. At the outset the predominating attitude favored negotiation and attempts toward compromise with avoidance of pressure tactics. A more recent trend, developing primarily after 1960, has seen compromise as unlikely and has favored a policy designed to force the South Africans into meeting their obligations.

Most attempts at compromise have faltered because of the Union's absolute refusal to put South West Africa under trusteeship and the U.N.'s equally stern refusal to permit incorporation of the mandate by the Union. While the Union government has expressed a willingness to accept reestablishment of the rights and obligations of the mandates system, the United Nations until 1950 would not even consider any settlement other than trusteeship for the region. The Union has suggested two possible solutions—conclusion of an international instrument to supervise the mandate with the three remaining Allied and Associated Powers, and partition of the area with part placed under trusteeship and part annexed to the Union of South Africa or administered as a strategic trust. The U.N. would not accept either of these proposals, and the situation again was deadlocked.

Complicating a settlement of the South West Africa issue is the fact that the case has not stood in isolation. South West Africa is a small target in two worldwide movements dedicated to the elimination of racial discrimination and colonialism. The policy of apartheid is the primary issue underlying the dispute. It is increasingly difficult for the African and Asian nations to make concessions on these questions, and for most of these states, there can be no compromise on apartheid.

Friction between the Union and the United Nations over issues other than the South West Africa dispute has increased the hostility of the Union government and reduced the likelihood of a compromise. The U.N. also has directly criticized racial policies within the Union, as well as within the mandate, and Union officials are aware that many U.N. members will not be satisfied unless apartheid within South Africa also is abandoned. In 1961 the General Assembly discussed four issues related to South Africa's racial policies, with only one of these relating to South West Africa. After the 1961 meeting the Union warned its European citizens in a *White Paper* that the four issues—the position of the Indians in the Union, the racial policies of the Union, the motion of censure, and the administration of South West Africa—all were related.[1] These incidents shaped opinion both within the United Nations and within the Union.

The South Africans think of themselves as the injured party. They claim the Union's 1946 report on its mandate was treated unjustly as a report from a trust area, and the members of the United Nations do not understand the problems which have faced the Union. The United Nations, by discussing the policy of apartheid and the treatment of Indians in South West Africa, has violated the domestic jurisdiction of that government, the Union charged.

Even after the 1950 court opinion that South Africa was not obligated legally to submit a trust agreement, many U.N. members still refused to consider any alternate arrangement, further hindering a compromise. Many resolutions submitted by this group continued to demand trusteeship for South West Africa.

While the official Union government never has proposed trusteeship as a solution, several members of the Union Parliament have. The vast majority of South African legislators support the policy of apartheid, but not all are convinced that it can be maintained

[1] Union of South Africa, *Report on the Proceedings at the Sixteenth Session of the General Assembly of the United Nations on Questions Affecting South Africa* (Pretoria: Government Printer, 1961), 1-48.

in the face of increasing opposition from the native population and from abroad. Also, some members of the small Labour and Liberal parties favor equal rights and opportunities for the natives.

For example, Dr. B. Friedman, a Parliament member, felt the Union was morally obligated to submit a trust agreement. The United Nations had established new principles, and the mandate could no longer be regarded as veiled annexation. A. T. Wanless of the Labour Party moved that the Union House of Assembly recognize that the rights of the League were vested in the United Nations and submit to U.N. supervision, with the proviso that the principle of direct representation for European and indirect representation for non-Europeans in the Union Parliament be recognized by the United Nations.[2] South Africa should submit a trust agreement asking that the area be administered as a fifth province of the Union. However, Wanless said it would be necessary on the grounds of justice to see that the African inhabitants of South West Africa were guarded against some of the repressive measures which the Union exercised against its own Africans.[3] The Union government never gave serious consideration to this plan for a combination trust area and fifth province, because after the court said South Africa did not have to submit a trust agreement, the officials saw no need for such action. However, it is doubtful that the General Assembly would have agreed to such an arrangement, since it still would not have granted sufficient control over the mandate to the United Nations.

In December, 1950, the General Assembly attempted to break the stalemate by establishing an *ad hoc* committee to supervise the administration of South West Africa and to negotiate with the Union. The committee was instructed that any agreements which were concluded must conform to the provisions of the 1950 advisory opinion.[4] This meant that the Union government must

[2] Union of South Africa, House of Assembly Debates, March 19, 1947, cols. 1366-72.

[3] South Africa House of Assembly Debates, April 11, 1947, cols, 2585-86.

[4] United Nations, General Assembly Resolutions, 5th Sess., Supp. No. 20, Res. 449A(V).

recognize that the rights and obligations of the mandate were still in force and must accept United Nations' supervision. Resulting from these discussions was a plan to reestablish the rights and obligations of the League Mandates System.

The Union agreed to sign an international agreement which would reestablish these obligations, but it would not accept the United Nations as a party to this agreement, nor would it agree to United Nations' supervision. The Union proposed to conclude this treaty with the three remaining Allied and Associated Powers—the United Kingdom, France, and the United States. Neither the United Nations nor the three Allied and Associated Powers would exercise a supervisory function. The agreement with the three nations would have a legal character, and supervision would be of a judicial nature. The Union government offered to accept the compulsory jurisdiction of the International Court of Justice if this jurisdiction were invoked by any two of the three Allied and Associated Powers.[5]

The Union government maintained that the agreement should be made with these three powers because sovereignty over the mandate had reverted to them when the League of Nations expired. Union authorities had not previously proposed this legal interpretation. They did not ask these three powers to terminate the mandate, and they never referred to the mandate of the United Kingdom, France, and the United States, always speaking of the Union's mandate. It would have proved interesting had these three powers claimed sovereignty over the mandate at this point. While the Allied and Associated Powers had assigned the mandates, all remaining functions had been performed by the League. The International Court of Justice had held that the rights and obligations of the League passed to the United Nations, not to these three countries.

There were a number of motives behind the Union's proposal, none of them the result of a legal interpretation. The repre-

[5] United Nations, Fourth Committee Records, 6th Sess. (Dec. 10, 1951), 136.

sentatives of the United Kingdom, France, and the United States had not been so outspoken against Union policies as had the African, Asian, and Communist states. The conclusion of such an agreement would have ended United Nations' debate and supervision, and the supervision provided by such an agreement would have been almost nonexistent. The Union would have accepted only a judicial supervision and would have limited the right to invoke that procedure to three powers when the court had advised that all members of the League enjoyed this right.

The *ad hoc* committee notified the Union government that it could not agree to this plan because it did not provide for a full implementation of the 1950 opinion. The court had established the right of the United Nations to supervise the administration of the mandate, and nothing less would be acceptable. The *ad hoc* committee did suggest an alternate proposal, which made several concessions to the Union government, suggesting the formation of a special committee of fifteen members, including the Union of South Africa, to exercise the functions of control formerly performed by the League Council. This committee would report to the United Nations.[6] Because this plan would have ensured United Nations supervision, the Union of South Africa rejected it.

Negotiations were reopened in 1952 by a second *ad hoc* group composed of representatives of Norway, Syria, Thailand, the United States, and Uruguay.[7] The composition of this committee was the same as the first except that a representative of the United Kingdom had been replaced by a delegate from Norway. After 1960 the committees established by the United Nations contained a larger number of African and Asian representatives who were less acceptable to Union officials than those of Europe and North and South America.[8] However, the effectiveness of these two

[6] Fourth Committee Records, 135-37.

[7] General Assembly Resolutions, 6th Sess., Res. 570A(VI).

[8] For example, the members of the Special Committee, appointed in 1960, were Australia, Cambodia, Ethiopia, India, Italy, Madagascar, Mali, Poland, Syria, Tanganyika, Tunisia, the Soviet Union, the United States, Uruguay, Venezuela, and Yugoslavia.

ad hoc groups was limited somewhat because the General Assembly also had assigned them the task of supervising the administration of the mandate.

During this second round of discussions Union representatives made additional concessions to the United Nations demands by agreeing that the final confirmation of the pact with the Allied and Associated Powers could rest with the United Nations. Moreover, the Union would make information available—information supplied as complete as that which had been submitted under the mandates system[9]—to those with whom the new agreement would be concluded.

The committee and the Union representatives had reached agreement on several important points: (1) that a new international instrument, which repeated with some minor alterations the principle of the "sacred trust" embodied in article two through five of the mandate agreement, should be concluded; (2) that information would be available; and (3) that there should be some form of supervision over the Union's administration. Here agreement ended, for two fundamental differences existed. The parties could not agree on how supervision should be carried out, nor on who should be the second party to the international agreement.[10] Negotiations continued, but these two points were never reconciled.

The Union government felt it could not afford to agree to supervision by a body so hostile to its administration. The Union's fear of supervision by the United Nations was illustrated well in a speech to the Union Parliament by Prime Minister Daniel Malan in 1954 in which he noted the Union's concessions in the offer to conclude an international agreement with the Allied and Associated Powers. Malan said the Union government would submit reports neither to the Allied and Associated Powers nor to the United Nations. The report submitted by General Smuts had

[9] United Nations, General Assembly, Annexes, 8th Sess., Agenda Item 36, pp. 3-4.
[10] General Assembly Annexes, 5.

resulted in a resolution opposing separate development for the Europeans and the non-Europeans. The time had come to protect the natives from the United Nations. "We would not submit reports to the U.N.O. if they asked us a hundred times, because they have interfered in our domestic affairs."[11]

In 1953 the General Assembly established the Committee on South West Africa which was to function according to the procedures followed by the Permanent Mandates Commission.[12] This should have made Union officials more responsive to United Nations overtures, but negotiations were still to be conducted within the limits established by the 1950 advisory opinion. The Union concluded that since the committee's terms of reference remained unchanged, there was no point in continuing discussions. Between 1953 and 1954 all contact between the Union government and the committee was broken.

In 1955 the South African officials informed the Committee on South West Africa that it saw no reason to renew discussions. Also during the tenth session, the Union government withdrew its delegation to the General Assembly and its permanent delegation to the United Nations because the U.N. established a political committee to inquire into racial discrimination in the Union of South Africa.[13]

In an attempt to reopen discussions with the South African government, the General Assembly established the Good Offices Committee composed of delegates from the United States, the United Kingdom, and Brazil, although some delegations in the General Assembly opposed this action. The October 25, 1957, resolution was passed by a vote of fifty to ten, with twenty abstentions. Most of the negative votes were cast by the Communist countries, and the abstentions were chiefly by the African and Asian nations.[14] These countries felt that further discussions were

[11] South Africa House of Assembly Debates, May 3, 1954, cols. 4486-87.
[12] General Assembly Resolutions, 8th Sess., Supp. No. 17, Res. 749A(VIII).
[13] Fourth Committee Records, 10th Sess. (503rd meeting), 195.
[14] Fourth Committee Records, 12th Sess. (Oct. 8, 1957), 59.

useless and that stronger measures should be applied to force South Africa to comply with the U.N.'s demands. The Good Offices Committee constituted several concessions to the Union government. Union representatives had expressed a desire to negotiate with the United States, the United Kingdom, and France; two of these countries were members of the committee. The terms of reference for this new committee were far less restrictive than those of its predecessors, because the Good Offices Committee was asked simply to conduct discussions toward finding a basis for an agreement to continue the international status of South West Africa.[15] This new group had still a third advantage over its predecessors in that it was not associated with the supervisory functions of the United Nations. These duties were to be retained by the Committee on South West Africa. The General Assembly was making one last effort to achieve a compromise settlement, and more than at any point in the history of the dispute, compromise seemed possible. The eventual failure of the Good Offices Committee to devise an acceptable solution resulted in disillusionment for all parties concerned. The Communist, Asian, and African states had proven their point that only more forceful measures would bring settlement.

In an almost complete reversal of previous policy, the South African government invited the members of the Good Offices Committee to visit South Africa and discuss a settlement of the dispute. During this discussion the committee did not offer any new suggestions, but repeated with one alteration the proposals of the second *ad hoc* committee: the Union should submit a trust agreement, or it should agree to the establishment of arrangements to reproduce within the United Nations a system corresponding to that of the League of Nations. The committee suggested establishing a commission resembling the Permanent Mandates Commission or a council composed only of those states which had been League members. Because the commission and the

[15] Fourth Committee Records, 64-65.

council would have been responsible to the United Nations, the Union refused to discuss these proposals.[16]

Another solution considered during the discussions was partition. This solution first had been suggested to the Committee on South West Africa in May, 1956, and had also been proposed by the Anti-Slavery Society of London.[17] The committee seemed somewhat favorable toward a proposal to permit South Africa to annex the areas of largest European settlement and to place the areas with predominantly nonwhite population under the Trusteeship system. Another alternative was to place the predominantly European region under trusteeship as a strategic trust. Many factors would have to be investigated before the region could be partitioned. For instance, the consent of the South West African population might have to be obtained. There likely would be a population exchange between the two areas. Many other economic, social, and political problems, of course, would also have to be resolved.[18]

At the conclusion of the talks, however, the Good Offices Committee recommended to the General Assembly that an investigation of the practicality of partition be carried out.

Louw, minister of external affairs for South Africa, assured the members of Committee Four that his government wished to conform to the new spirit of conciliation. He said the proposal for partition was the most practical suggestion made thus far, and he further explained that the General Assembly was not being asked to approve partition, but merely to invite the Union authorities to investigate such a plan.[19]

All semblance of conciliation between the Union and the United Nations ended, however, when Committee Four voted to grant oral hearings to Michael Scott and Kerina Getzen. The Union

[16] General Assembly Annexes, 13th Sess., Agenda Item 39, pp. 1-9.

[17] United Nations, *Report of the Committee on South West Africa,* 11th Sess., Supp. No. 12 (A/3151, 1956), 28-29.

[18] General Assembly Annexes, 13th Sess., Agenda Item 39, pp. 1-9.

[19] Fourth Committee Records, 13th Sess. (Sept. 26, 1958), 3-8.

delegation had withdrawn from Committee Four in 1949 and from the General Assembly in 1951 because oral petitioners had been heard. Louw stated that the actions of the Committee Four confirmed his government's belief that the United Nations was being used as a forum for waging propaganda and ideological warfare against the Union. It was apparent that a number of delegates had come to the Committee Four prepared to wreck the work of the Good Offices Committee. Because of Committee Four's decision to hear the two oral petitions, the Union once again withdrew its delegation from the Committee Four.[20]

If the South Africans were sincere in their offer to investigate partition, why did the representatives walk out of the Committee Four meetings? South Africa might have secured annexation of the police zone, which contained most of the wealth and the majority of the European population. The Union officials possibly withdrew because they had concluded that the United Nations would never approve such an agreement.

When Louw later reviewed these discussions for the Union House of Assembly, he noted that the Union delegation had made concessions to the United Nations and that the Union Government had acted in good faith. He stated that the Union had refused to accept the proposal to reestablish the mandates system because reports would have to be submitted to the United Nations. The Union, however, had promised to consider partition and had even recognized that South West Africa possessed an "international charter." The government had not agreed to the international status prescribed by the International Court of Justice, but it had recognized its "international character." Louw said that it soon became clear that a large majority had come to Committee Four meetings determined to wreck the work of the Good Offices Committee. A report by this committee had been published in India, Ghana, and other areas before it was presented to Committee Four. If the Union representatives had not walked

20 Fourth Committee Records, 23-27.

out in opposition to the hearing of oral reports, the Union would have lost face.[21]

It is quite probable that a majority of the members of Committee Four had ruled out partition and saw no need to investigate the proposal, for it involved greater concessions than these members were willing to make. As Michael Scott had said, the partitioning of South West Africa would in fact be an act of apartheid. The African inhabitants of that part of the territory placed under trusteeship would still be governed by apartheid, and it would be difficult for the United Nations to protect the rights of the peoples in the trust area. The natives would remain dependent upon employment within police zone or in the Union of South Africa where pass laws were in force.[22] Taken as a whole, South West Africa does not constitute a logical economic unit, and the economically poorer area of the north would remain dependent upon the rest of the territory. Acceptance of partition not only would have been a loss of face, but it would also have been a breach of trust. While the representatives of the United Kingdom, the United States, and Brazil were willing to discuss such a settlement, a majority of the General Assembly was not. Many of the African, Asian, and Communist countries had opposed these negotiations from the outset, and they were not going to accept a solution which they regarded as a complete defeat.

The United Kingdom and the Commonwealth nations, the United States, and a number of the Latin American nations had led the movement favoring compromise. Chief opposition to negotiations and compromise had emanated from the Soviet bloc and from a group of the African and Asian nations. Both the United Kingdom and the Soviet countires had based their positions on legal grounds. The United Kingdom stressed the portion of the 1950 advisory opinion that the Union was not legally obligated to submit a trust agreement. Therefore, this group had reasoned, the

[21] South Africa House of Assembly Debates, May 11, 1959, cols. 5563-67.
[22] Fourth Committee Records, 13th Sess. (Oct. 6, 1958), 31.

Union government was free to choose a means for implementing the remainder of the opinion. The Soviet nations did not accept the 1950 opinion, and they maintained that South West Africa must either be placed under the trusteeship system or granted full independence.

SEVEN:

TOWARD A MORE FORCEFUL POLICY

By 1960 the members of the United Nations were tired of the compromise approach, and they embarked on a more forceful course. This new policy was reflected by the institution of contentious proceedings by Ethiopia and Liberia before the International Court of Justice; the General Assembly's authorization of a factfinding mission to South West Africa; the designation of the situation in South West Africa as a threat to international peace and security; and the passage of measures designed to establish United Nations presence in South West Africa.

A number of factors apparently contributed to this change in policy. The repeated refusal of the Union of South Africa to recognize the right of the United Nations to supervise its administration and its failure to assist any of the United Nations committees in this supervisory effort caused U.N. members to favor a more forceful policy. In spite of the intensified effort, the supervision established was no better than that afforded by the League. The United Nations had an obligation to achieve that much. If the Union had nothing to hide, there was no reason not to supply information, the members believed. A second contributing factor was the failure of negotiations between several United Nations groups and the Union of South Africa. If years of quiet discussion and constant urging could not bring about a settlement, perhaps sterner measures were necessary, some U.N. members reasoned.

A third factor contributing to the increasing impatience of the United Nations involved the changed composition of the General Assembly. Between 1946 and 1966 the membership of the United Nations more than doubled. The majority of the 67 new members were the newly independent Asian and African nations strongly opposed to colonialism and racial discrimination. This group has been in the forefront of the attack against the Union. Also, the Communist countries of the United Nations, led by Russia, have not let pass the opportunity to influence favorably this group. For various reasons, ultimately most United Nations members were forced into a position opposing the Union. There is no legal or moral defense for the policy of apartheid, and no leading nation can afford to defend it. When nations vote or abstain seemingly in favor of the Union of South Africa, they usually have based their votes upon legal objections to the actions proposed. Such countries as Britain, Australia, New Zealand, Belgium, France, and the United States occasionally have done this. Britain was caught in a delicate situation until the new Republic of South Africa withdrew from the Commonwealth of Nations on May 31, 1961. In attempting to hold the Commonwealth together, the British were caught between the South African position and the position held by the majority of the Commonwealth members. After the Republic's withdrawal, the British had more freedom of action, although no actual reversal in their voting on the South West Africa issue occurred. Their position had been dictated by a legal interpretation which they felt was correct. A change in British attitude was revealed, however, in speeches which were more critical of South African policies. Today South Africa is practically without a friend in the United Nations. In the efforts of this international organization to bring the South West Africa dispute to an acceptable conclusion, time is on the side of the South African native. In this revolutionary age South Africa's policies are untenable.

The United Nations decided to make no major decisions concerning the future status of South West Africa until it received the court's decision in the case brought by Ethiopia and Liberia, but it did decide by a vote of eighty-two to one, with nine abstentions, to continue its consideration of the case. South Africa attempted to end all United Nations debate and action on the South West Africa issue by arguing that the case was *sub judice*. The rule of *sub judice* provides that a court may not be hindered in any way in the impartial exercise of its functions while a case is pending before the court. B. G. Fourie, a Union delegate, moved that debate on the issue within the United Nations be ended, because Fourie said public comment of any kind on issues pending in such a court, including decisions or recommendations by public bodies, is regarded as likely to impede or to embarrass the court in the exercise of its judicial functions.[1] The General Assembly is empowered to discuss any matter within the scope of the United Nations charter with the one exception of those currently under consideration by the Security Council. Not only did the General Assembly continue to debate the case, but the tone of its resolutions became increasingly belligerent. However, because the case was pending before the court, the General Assembly pursued a more moderate course than it otherwise might have chosen. For example, all proposals to enforce economic sanctions against South Africa failed to receive a two-thirds majority vote, partly because many members said the United Nations should not embark upon such a course until the court made its decision.

Although the General Assembly refrained from applying force in South West Africa, its resolutions anticipated a favorable verdict from the court. Through the passage of forceful resolutions, the General Assembly tried to establish a United Nations presence in South West Africa. Thus far, the General Assembly has not chosen to back its strong words with strong measures. In 1957 the General Assembly demanded that the government of the Union of South Africa: (1) transfer government responsibility to representative institutions of the territory of South West Africa; (2) revise existing policies and practices of native administration in accordance with the spirit of the mandate; (3) extend representation in the existing territorial legislature to all inhabitants; (4) base public employment on qualifications other than race; (5) train non-Europeans for higher posts in the administration; (6) discontinue residential restrictions based on the policy of apartheid; (7) repeal laws of the territory having discriminatory restrictions; and

[1] United Nations, General Assembly, Plenary Meetings, 15th Sess., II (Dec. 18, 190), 1385-87.

(8) eliminate racial discrimination from the educational system.[2] Unfortunately, this resolution was not backed by force, and it was ignored.

During the sixteenth session of the General Assembly the members tried a different approach to the problem by attempting to establish special programs to train as many South West African natives as possible in skills and administration in such vital areas as economics, law, and health. U.N. members were asked to contribute funds to a special fellowship program, and specialized agencies of the United Nations were asked to give technical aid.[3] Again the Union did not cooperate, refusing assistance from the specialized agencies and denying passports to natives for the purposes of studying abroad.

During the same session, the Special Committee for South West Africa was asked to (1) visit South West Africa before May 1, 1962; (2) see that South Africa's military forces were evacuated; (3) secure the release of all political prisoners; (4) secure the repeal of all laws and regulations related to the policy of apartheid; (5) prepare for general elections to be held under United Nations supervision; and (6) advise and assist the government put in power by these elections in preparing the territory for full independence.[4] This resolution, sponsored by thirty-five of the Afro-Asian nations, was probably the most inclusive demand passed by the General Assembly. While the resolution was characterized by forceful language, the General Assembly was once more assuming that the Union would cooperate with the committee or at least would not prevent it from carrying out its duties. South Africa did agree to allow the chairman and vice-chairman of the committee to visit South West Africa, but the remaining members were refused admittance, and none of the provisions of the resolution were carried out.

A later resolution, actually an admission of the General Assem-

<hr/>

[2] United Nations, General Assembly Resolutions, 11th Sess., Supp. No. 17, Res. 1054(XI).

[3] General Assembly Resolutions, 16th Sess., Supp. No. 17, Res. 1705(XVI).

[4] General Assembly Resolutions, 16th Sess., Supp. No. 17, Res. 1702(XVI).

bly's failure, did not order a committee to carry out specific tasks, but merely urged the Union of South Africa to refrain from taking direct or indirect actions to prevent the provisions of past resolutions from being carried out.[5] The African, Asian, and Communist nations generally have favored the use of economic sanctions to force the Union to conform to the demands of the U.N. In 1960, Ghana unilaterally established an economic boycott against the Union of South Africa because of the Union's policy of apartheid. The delegate from Ghana said that Africa would not sit by indefinitely and do nothing about the policies of South Africa. Africans would use force if necessary, and the time would come when the world would join them.[6] The nations of Western Europe and North and South America have not yet been willing to apply any types of sanctions, and the United Nations had been unsuccessful in establishing its presence in South West Africa.

At one point the United Nations authorized a factfinding mission to South West Africa to be carried out with or without the cooperation of the Union of South Africa.[7] This came subsequent to the submission of the South West Africa case to the International Court of Justice in 1960. Despite objections that this mission violated the principle of *sub judice* and overstepped the powers granted by the mandate, the General Assembly approved it by a two-thirds majority. The United Nations charter allows for such factfinding missions, but this had not been a practice of the Permanent Mandates Commission. The Union warned that if the committee members entered the mandate they would be arrested, because the Union had the right to refuse visas to the area.[8]

Since the committee was denied permission to enter the mandate, its members decided to visit other African nations and interview exiles from South West Africa. In Ghana, their first stop,

[5] General Assembly Resolutions, 17th Sess., Supp. No. 17, Res. 1805(XVII).
[6] United Nations, Fourth Committee Records, 16th Sess., I (Nov. 28, 1961), 443-58.
[7] General Assembly Resolutions, 15th Sess., Supp. No. 16, Res. 1568(XV).
[8] Fourth Committee Records, 16th Sess., I (Nov. 21, 1961), 381-82.

they were told by exiles that if the United Nations did not soon find a solution to the South West African problem, there would be bloodshed. While in Ghana the committee members decided to enter South West Africa without the permission of the Union government. After refugees told the committee that a military force of 4,000 men had been stationed along the border to prevent its entry, the committee resumed its original plan to travel from Ghana to Bechuanaland. Because the committee refused to promise that they would not cross into South West Africa from Bechuanaland, the British government withdrew permission for the group to enter that territory. Instead, the committee traveled to Tanganyika. As a result of the information gathered on this tour, the members of the Committee on South West Africa concluded that the United Nations must take more forceful actions in South West Africa—including the use of compulsive measures to expel South Africa from the mandate if violence was to be avoided.[9]

While the Union of South Africa would not allow the United Nations committee to visit South West Africa, it did invite the three former presidents of the General Assembly to visit. The Union said the tour of these three persons could ascertain that there existed no threat to international peace and security. The report of this group would not be submitted to the United Nations, but to the Union government. Union authorities would then release the report in its entirety.[10] The General Assembly, however, did not trust Union representatives with the compilation of such a report and instead, it created the Special Committee for South West Africa and assigned it to visit the mandate and see that laws related to apartheid were repealed.[11]

South African officials refused to receive the entire committee, but the chairman and vice-chairman were invited to visit Pretoria,

[9] United Nations, *Report of the Committee on South West Africa Con-*
ing the Implementation of General Assembly Resolution 1568(XV), 16th
Sess., Supp. No. 12A (A/4926, 1961), 3-22.
[10] Fourth Committee Records, 16th Sess., I (Nov. 21, 1961), 381-82.
[11] General Assembly Resolutions, 16th Sess., Supp. No. 17, Res. 1702(XVI).

South Africa. After a visit to the Union, if the committee felt it necessary, a visit to South West Africa could be arranged. The Union claimed that the entire committee was not being invited because such action might prejudice the Union's position before the International Court. Also, Union officials stated that this invitation was not to be interpreted as a recognition of United Nations authority over the mandate.[12] This was the first time that any representatives of the United Nations had been permitted to visit the mandated territory.

The officials visited South Africa and South West Africa from May 4 to May 28, 1962, but what actually happened remains somewhat mysterious. The visiting officials later denied many of the statements released and attributed to them during the period of their tour. For example, Victorio D. Carpio of the Philippines, chairman of the committee, was quoted as saying that he saw no signs of slavery, genocide, or military occupation. While the whites had done much for the nonwhites, the United Nations could do much more in housing, education, and economic development. Mr. Carpio supposedly said at a private luncheon that he would like to see apartheid succeed. Later he denied having made these statements.

On May 26, a communique from the South African government said two members of the committee had rejected charges that conditions in South West Africa constituted a threat to international peace and found no proof that the territory was being militarized or that the natives were being exterminated.[13] Three weeks later Carpio said he had no part in the communique and, in fact, had been ill and confined in bed at the time the report was prepared. The vice-chairman of the committee, Martinez de Alva of Mexico, said, however, that Carpio had acquiesced fully to the statement.[14] There was some speculation that the

[12] United Nations, Report of the Special Committee for South West Africa, 17th Sess., Supp. No. 12 (A/3625, 1957), 1-3.

[13] "United Nations Representatives Visit," *Africa Digest*, X (Aug., 1962), 27-28.

[14] *New York Times*, Aug. 10, 1962, p. 3.

Philippine chairman had reversed his opinion after the visit because he subsequently was appointed ambassador to the United Arab Republic, a strong critic of Union policy in South West Africa.[15]

Regardless of what happened in Pretoria, the chairman and vice-chairman reported to the United Nations that their visit to the mandated territory had convinced them that the administration of South West Africa was pervaded by the rigorous application of apartheid in all aspects of life of the African population. The administration of the area was contradictory to the principles and purposes of the mandate, they said. The two reported that while the leaders of European groups in the territory generally opposed United Nations interference, most of the native leaders expressed a strong desire to have the United Nations administer South West Africa.[16] The committee was largely unsuccessful in carrying out the duties assigned to it by the General Assembly. Union officials refused to discuss the repeal of laws relating to apartheid, denied that there were any political prisoners in South West Africa, refused to cooperate with plans for natives to study abroad, and refused to accept aid from the specialized agencies of the United Nations.

In the contentious proceedings filed with the International Court of Justice on November 4, 1960, Ethiopia and Liberia charged the Union with violations of its duties as the mandatory of South West Africa and invoked the compulsory jurisdiction of the court. This decision to ask the court to render a binding verdict on South African administration was not made in haste. It began in February, 1957, when the General Assembly requested that the Committee on South West Africa investigate legal means which were open to the bodies or to the members of the United Nations to insure that the Union of South Africa fulfilled the obligations of the mandate.[17] The committee replied that additional advisory opinions could be sought on supervisory functions, or on whether

15 *New York Times,* June 10, 1962, p. 2.
16 Special Committee Report, 17th Sess., Supp. No. 12, p. 7.
17 General Assembly Resolutions, 11th Sess., Supp. No. 17, Res. 1060(XI).

specific acts of the Union government conformed with the obligations of the mandate. The committee also concluded that the
right to bring contentious proceedings against the Union rested
with all members of the United Nations. The 1950 advisory
opinion did not state that any member of the United Nations
could invoke the compulsory jurisdiction of the court, but the
court had not been requested to rule on that point. Regardless of
the correct position, the committee concluded that there was little
doubt that nations which were members of the League at the
date of its dissolution and were now members of the United
Nations enjoyed this right.[18]

The General Assembly wanted a more specific reply, and it
asked the committee to formulate a list of questions which would
be suitable to submit to the court for advisory opinions.[19] The
committee listed two groups of acts on which the court could be
consulted. The first category, which was related to the international
status of South West Africa, included the questions about South
West Africa's representation in the Union Parliament and the
degree and nature of the integration of the mandate with the
Union of South Africa. The second category of questions related
to the moral and material well-being and the social progress of the
inhabitants of the territory. The General Assembly could ask the
court if such policies as the application of apartheid to South West
Africa, the application of racially-discriminatory legislation, aliena-
tion and allocation of lands, and legislation providing for the
expulsion from the area of persons under the protection of the
mandates system were in conformity with the international obligations of the Union of South Africa. These questions could be
put to the court specifically, or the court could be asked to rule in
terms of the compatibility of overall Union policy.[20] The General
Assembly did not seek further advisory opinions, but these actions
provided the groundwork for the suit by Ethiopia and Liberia.

[18] Special Committee Report, 12th Sess., Supp. No. 12A, pp. 3-5.
[19] General Assembly Resolutions, 12th Sess., Supp. No. 18, Res. 1142 (XII).
[20] Report of the Committee on South West Africa, 13th Sess., Supp. No.
12 (A/3906, 1958), 7.

The immediate stimulus for the suit was a decision made at the Second Conference of Independent African States, which met at Addis Ababa, Ethiopia. A later General Assembly resolution, however, endorsed that conference's conclusion that the dispute between the Union and the United Nations could not be settled by negotiation and that the Union had failed to uphold its obligations under the mandate.[21]

The suit charged the Union government with pursuing policies which grossly violated the Union's duties under the mandate agreement. Specifically, the Union was accused of suppressing the rights and liberties of the inhabitants of South West Africa in the following ways: limiting the franchise to persons of European descent; refusing to grant equal access to education according to merit, and depriving native children of adequate educational facilities; segregating residential areas by law according to race or tribal origin; forbidding trade union membership to non-Europeans; excluding natives from numerous occupations; subjecting employees to criminal penalty for breaching terms of employment; requiring natives to possess a pass to travel beyond the confines of a particular location, reserve, farm, or place of employment; denying grants or leases of land to native Asians and colored persons; subjecting natives to curfew orders; forcing deportation at the discretion of the administration of the territory without right of appeal or judicial review; prohibiting native membership to political parties; and refusing to transmit petitions and annual reports to the United Nations. The applicants requested that the court order that the Union of South Africa cease to practice apartheid in the territory and insist that the Union government submit reports and petitions to the United Nations.[22]

South Africa immediately disputed the jurisdiction of the International Court and submitted preliminary objections based upon four major legal points. The Union maintained that the mandate for South West Africa had never been, or at least since the

[21] General Assembly Resolutions, 15th Sess., Supp. No. 16, Res. 1565(XV).
[22] New York Times, Nov. 5, 1960, p. 1.

dissolution of the League was no longer, a treaty in force within the meaning of article 37 of the Statute of the Court. The Union's lawyers argued that the mandate had taken the form of a resolution and that the rights and obligations in relation to the administration of South West Africa still existed, because they were of an objective character. However, the rights and obligations relating to the supervision of the territory had expired with the League. The Union government also argued that article 7 of the mandate agreement, by which the Permanent Court of Justice had jurisdiction over certain types of disputes, was no longer in force, because it had been of a contractual nature. When the International Court of Justice handed down its preliminary decision on this point, it upheld the interpretation given in the 1950 advisory opinion. All the rights and obligations of the mandate were still in force, and the International Court of Justice was the successor to the rights of the Permanent Court of Justice. This legal argument was extremely weak, because the mandate agreement constituted a binding international treaty.

The Union government also entered a technical objection, based upon the wording of article 7 of the mandate agreement. Article 7 stated that another member of the League of Nations could invoke the compulsory jurisdiction of the court. South Africa maintained that since there was no longer a League, there were no longer any members of the League. This point also had been considered in the 1950 advisory opinion, and the court concluded that as long as the respondent held to the right to administer the territory, members of the League could invoke the compulsory jurisdiction of the court. Both Ethiopia and Liberia had been members of the League of Nations.

The third objection raised by the Union was that the present case was not a dispute as envisaged by article 7 of the mandate. The court ruled that the case constituted a dispute, because the members of the League had a legal right or interest in the mandatory's observance of its obligations to both the inhabitants of the mandate and to the League of Nations. The fourth objection, which was related to the third, stated that if a dispute did exist, it was of such a nature that it could be settled by negotiations. There had never been direct negotiation between the Union and Ethiopia and Liberia. The court reasoned that a deadlock existed even though direct negotiations had never taken place, because both Ethiopia and Liberia had participated in seeking a settlement through the United Nations.

By a vote of eight to seven, the court decided that a dispute existed and that it was suitable for adjudication.[23] The narrow margin of this December 21, 1962, preliminary decision is difficult to explain, especially since the court in its 1950 advisory opinion already had decided two of the points in this case. The composition of the court had changed drastically since 1950, however. According to article 31, paragraph 3 of the statute of the court, each party to a dispute may choose a judge to sit as a member of the court, provided no judge of its own nationality already is in the court. Judges sit as individuals rather than as representatives of states, a provision designed to ensure the court's impartiality. Ethiopia and Liberia selected Sir Louis Mbanefo of Nigeria, and South Africa chose Jacques Theodore Van Wyk of the appellate division of the Supreme Court of South Africa.

In the preliminary decision Judges R. J. Alfaro, A. H. Badawi, L. M. Moreno Quintana, J. K. Wellington, Vladimir M. Koretsky, Jose Luis Duspamente y Rivero, Philip Jessup, and Sir Louis Mbanefo cast affirmative votes; the dissenting votes were cast by Judges D. Winiarski, J. Basdevant, Jean Spiropoulox, Perry C. Spender, Sir Gerald Fitzmaurice, Gaetano Morelli, and J. T. Van Wyk.[24] Judges Winiarski and Basdevant sat on the court in 1950, and Winiarski, Basdevant, Badawi, and Moreno Quintana were members of the court when the 1955 and 1956 advisory opinions were issued. The 1955 decision on voting procedure had been unanimous. In 1956 Judge Winiarski agreed that the hearing of oral petitions was not inconsistent with the 1950 opinion, while Badawi, Basdevant, and Moreno Quintana dissented.

[23] "Preliminary Judgment on South West Africa," *United Nations Review,* X (Feb., 1963), 66-69.
[24] *New York Times,* Dec. 22, 1962, p. 2.

The most significant difference between this case and the previous court judgments was that this time the court was being asked to issue a binding decision rather than just an advisory opinion. The court held the legal power either to grant the United Nations total jurisdiction over South West Africa or to undermine the United Nations' position entirely. A ruling that the Union was no longer competent to administer South West Africa would remove legal barriers to United Nations intervention, and the U.N. would be free to send observers, teachers, doctors, technicians, and such to aid the natives of the territory.

Most U.N. members believed that the court had only two alternatives in the South West African dispute—to agree in whole or in part with either Ethiopia and Liberia or with South Africa. But by basing the decision on a legal technicality and by reversing portions of its earlier advisory opinions and its preliminary decision, the court found a third alternative which resolved nothing and led the African nations to charge that the court was a useless tool in resolving the racial grievances of the Africans.

The first question the court had to resolve was whether a legal dispute suitable for adjudication did exist and whether Ethiopia and Liberia were competent to bring suit. On July 18, 1966, the court by a vote of eight to seven decided that Liberia and Ethiopia had "no legal interest" in the case and that the court, therefore, would not rule on the substantive issues of the case. The court's vote had split seven to seven with President Percy Spender of Australia casting a second vote to break the tie.[25] The decision might well have gone the other way if Judge Abdel H. Badawi of the United Arab Republic had not died the year before. The court normally is composed of fifteen judges, but no successor for Badawi had been chosen prior to the decision.

Supporting the majority decision were Judges Gaetano Morelli of Italy, Bohdan Winiarski of Poland, Jean Spiropoulox of Greece, Andre Gros of France, Gerald Fitzmaurice of Britain, and J. T. Van Wyk of South Africa. Dissenting votes were cast by Philip C. Jessup of the United States, V. K. Wellington Koo of Nation-

25 *New York Times,* July 19, 1966, p. 1.

alist China, Vladimir M. Koretsky of the Soviet Union, Kotaro
Tanaka of Japan, Luis Padilla Nervo of Mexico, Isaac Forster of
Senegal and Louis Mbanefo, the *ad hoc* judge named by Liberia
and Ethiopia.[26] Of the nine judges who were members of the
court when the preliminary decision was delivered none reversed
his original opinion. In the preliminary and final judgments Judges
Winiarski, Spiropoulox, Spender, Fitzmaurice, Morelli, and Van
Wyk voted not to entertain the suit, and Judges Koretsky, Jessup,
and Mbanefo voted that the court had jurisdiction.

The dismissal on a technicality came after ninety-nine separate
sessions of debate, spanning six years, and after the issuance of a
2,900-page report.[27] The basis for the decision was that the mandate made no provision for the individual members to challenge its
execution. Article 2 of the Covenant of the League of Nations
provided that the "actions of the League under this Covenant
shall be effected through the instrumentality of an Assembly and
of a Council with a permanent Secretariat." The court said the
mandatories were to be agents of the League and not of each and
every member of it individually.[28] Referring to humanitarian
arguments put forward by the complainants, the court said it was
necessary not to confuse the moral ideal with the legal rules.
While the decision apparently blocked any further suit on the
issue in the court under its existing statute, the decision did not
reverse sections of the advisory opinions granting supervisory
rights over the mandate to the United Nations.

Philip Jessup of the United States filed a 129-page dissent which
charged that the court's decision was unfounded in law and was a
misconception "of the peace settlement at the close of World War
I, and of the nature and functioning of the League of Nations."
Referring to earlier decisions, Jessup said that the court had swept
away its record of sixteen years. The court's view "must be one
which takes account of the views and attitudes of the contemporary
community." Jessup felt that the accumulation of expressions

[26] *New York Times,* July 19, 1966, p. 17.
[27] "Shock from the Hague," *Newsweek,* Aug. 1, 1966, pp. 42-47.
[28] *New York Times,* July 19, 1966, p. 16.

condemning apartheid were proof of the pertinent contemporary international standard.[29]

Although the court's deliberations were not aimed primarily at judging the quality of South Africa's administration of its mandate, additional information about conditions in South West Africa was revealed, touching off new debate. Ernest A. Gross, chief counsel to Ethiopia and Liberia, stated that the court hearings revealed that in more than forty years of Union administration little had been done for the South African native. No natives had qualified in the professions of law, medicine, engineering, dentistry, or registered nursing. Still in effect were regulations preventing natives from joining labor unions with the right of collective bargaining. Other restrictions on natives included barring them from skilled occupations, enforcing the pass system, and maintaining native residence locations. Perhaps most importantly, natives still had no voice in government and in the administration of their affairs.[30]

Conversely, S. T. Possony, director of the international political studies program of the Hoover Institute for War, Revolution, and Peace, charged that the Union was not the only nation with laws discriminating on the basis of race, religion, or sex. Testifying before the court in the behalf of South Africa, Possony said that at least fifty states of the world, among them Ethiopia and Liberia, had such laws.[31] A crucial point developing in the debate was not whether discrimination was imposed, but by whom it was imposed —an African majority or a European minority.

One only can speculate about what action the United Nations might have taken had the decision been different and what action it now will take. Had the decision been directly in favor of South Africa, the basic arguments of the United Nations would have been destroyed. The United Nations case against South Africa has been founded on three arguments. First, South Africa, even

[29] New York Times, July 19, 1966, pp. 1, 17.

[30] Ernest A. Gross, "The South West Africa Case: What Happened?" Foreign Affairs (Oct., 1966), 41.

[31] Jacobs, A Special Study of South West Africa in Law and Politics, 12-13.

though it is not legally obligated to do so, by every moral principle should place South West Africa under trusteeship. Second, South Africa is legally obligated to submit to United Nations supervision and to transmit reports and petitions. Finally, and most importantly, the virtual annexation of the mandate and the application of apartheid to the area are gross violations of the provisions of the mandate. If the court had backed the United Nations on the question of supervision as it did in 1950, but not on the questions about apartheid, the decision would have been essentially meaningless. If it were not for the question of apartheid, it is likely that the question of supervision could have been settled by negotiation long ago. If apartheid had not existed and if the people of South West Africa had expressed such a desire, it is probable that the United Nations would have approved the incorporation of the mandate with South Africa. Such a settlement would have been geographically and economically logical. At this point, however, the members of the United Nations would have received little satisfaction in supervising a territory in which the practice of apartheid with all its associated evils was supported by a legally binding decision of the International Court of Justice. In effect, if the court failed to agree with Ethiopia and Liberia on all points, it might as well have disagreed completely.

If the court had agreed with Ethiopia and Liberia that South Africa had violated the provisions of its mandate, the course of the United Nations still would have been difficult. The decision of the court not necessarily would have determined the future relationship between South West Africa and the United Nations. The court was asked to determine only whether the Republic of South Africa had violated the provisions of its mandate and whether the Republic was legally entitled to continue its administration of that territory. The status to be accorded South West Africa following this decision would have to be determined by the United Nations, not the court. Several alternative courses were available but the status actually given the territory might well have depended upon the Republic's reaction to the decision.

Most likely, the court and the United Nations would have given the Republic government a specified time period in which to bring their administration into accord with the obligations of the mandate. If South Africa did not comply with these demands, the issue likely would have been brought before the Security Council. The council might have tried to force compliance by using economic and military sanctions, or it might have decided that South Africa was no longer entitled to administer the territory. Unfortunately, either policy might have required the use of force. Also, the financial difficulties and the peacekeeping operations of the United Nations might have limited U.N. involvement in South West Africa.

If the court's decision had empowered the United Nations to revoke South Africa's mandate over South West Africa, the U.N. still would have been faced with the problem of deciding how the territory would be governed. There were a number of possibilities. South West Africa could have been placed under the United Nations Trusteeship System with a nation other than the Republic of South Africa acting as administrator. If this had been the case, it might have been difficult to find a nation both capable and willing to administer the area. It is unfortunate that the Republic has refused to cooperate with the United Nations, for South Africa country is the logical administrator of the territory. Another possibility would have been for the United Nations to establish a trust agreement with the U.N. itself acting as administrator. A third alternative would have been to grant the territory's independence, backed by a guarantee by the United Nations of its continued separate existence. Although some nations, particularly the new African states, desire the immediate independence of all dependent areas, independence is not the most desirable solution. During German and South African rule of the territory there has been no preparation for self-government. So entwined is the economy of South West Africa with that of the Republic that the territory could not be sustained economically without considerable outside assistance.

Perhaps the best solution would have been either for the Republic to have abandoned apartheid and ruled the area according to the provisions of the mandate or for the U.N. to have placed the territory under trusteeship. South Africa would not likely have adopted either of these courses, however. Even if South African officials had been willing to make some concessions, the members of the United Nations likely would have been skeptical. The only real alternative was for the United Nations to render aid to South West Africa under some form of trusteeship.

Many U.N. members feared that the court's decision would precipitate an immediate crisis in South West Africa. As the court's decision drew near, it became increasingly obvious that a split concerning how tough a policy should be applied toward South Africa had developed among the members of the United Nations. The United States and Britain were trying to avoid a major crisis by pleading for restraint on the part of the African nations and by urging South Africa to refrain from applying apartheid in South West Africa. While not wishing to alienate the African states, the United States was naturally hesitant to become involved militarily in another area at a time when involvement in Vietnam continued. The British apparently feared that the South West Africa situation could complicate their policy toward Rhodesia. The Russians, however, have continued their moral support of the African position.

The decision of the court averted an immediate crisis, but the situation eventually may become more explosive. The court's verdict must be viewed as a victory for South Africa, and it undoubtedly has strengthened South Africa's resistance to reform. The African nations reacted to the court's verdict with bewilderment and bitterness, charging that the court refused to consider the merits of the case because it involved a touchy political issue. These nations concluded that the court was of no value in their struggle against colonialism and racism.

The decision also has brought criticism of the structure of the court. Although the court supposedly is composed of individuals rather than representatives of states, some United Nations delegates are now advocating an enlargement of the court's membership so that the distinct geographical regions of the world are reflected in the composition of the court in the same proportion as they are in the General Assembly.[32] Ernest A. Gross feels that serious consideration should be given to amending the statute of the court to enable the United Nations to appear as a party in appropriate cases before the court. To preclude this body from seeking a binding decision in a dispute to which it is a party creates a dangerous vacuum in the process of peaceful settlement of world problems.[33]

Despite the court's decision, the majority of United Nations members have not been diverted from their goal of independence for South West Africa. They have proceeded upon the bases that the United Nations still has the legal right to supervise South West Africa's administration and that the situation within the territory constitutes a threat to international peace and security. Subsequent to the court's decision, an eight-nation steering committee was established to determine what action could be taken against South Africa.

On October 27, 1966, in a surprising move, the General Assembly adopted a resolution terminating South Africa's mandate for South West Africa and declaring that South Africa had no other right to administer the territory, which would now come under the direct responsibility of the United Nations. This resolution, sponsored by fifty-four Afro-Asian powers and amended by nineteen Latin American states plus Trinidad and Tobago, and Jamaica, was adopted by a vote of one hundred fourteen to two (Portugal and South Africa), with three abstentions (France, Malawi, and the United Kingdom).[34] An *ad hoc* committee of fourteen members (Canada, Chile, Czechoslovakia, Ethiopia, Finland, Italy, Japan, Mexico, Nigeria, Pakistan, Senegal, the Soviet Union, the United Arab Republic and the United States) was established to recom-

[32] United Nations, *Monthly Chronicle* (Oct., 1966), 16.
[33] Gross, *Foreign Affairs* (Oct., 1966), 47.
[34] *Monthly Chronicle* (Nov., 1966), 20.

mend practical means by which South West Africa should be administered to enable the natives to exercise the right of self-determination and to achieve independence.[35]

Prior to the adoption of this resolution, the United States sponsored a subamendment which called for the termination of the mandate, but asked that the United Nations preserve the international status of the territory instead of making it a direct responsibility of the United Nations. This amendment failed by a vote of eighteen for, fifty-two against, with forty-nine abstentions. While the United States supported the majority resolution, the French abstained on the ground that they had reservations about the legality of this action. South Africa warned the United Nations that attempts from the outside to impose a dangerous and unwanted system would be resisted by South Africa with all the forces at its command. The United Nations should not be turned into an instrument of aggression.[36]

The *ad hoc* committee for South West Africa concluded its meetings on March 31, 1967, and forwarded its recommendations to the special session of the General Assembly which opened on April 21. The committee failed to reach agreement and recommended to the General Assembly that it adopt one of three proposals which had been submitted to the committee. The most extreme suggestion, introduced by Ethiopia, Nigeria, Senegal, and the United Arab Republic, provided for the creation of a council which would assume responsibility for the administration of South West Africa, supervise the withdrawal of South African police and military personnel, and replace these officials with U.N. representatives, many of whom would be drawn from the indigenous population. This program lists June, 1968, as the target date for independence and would be financed by revenue collected in the territory, by voluntary funds, and from the regular U.N. budget. If the South African government should resist this transfer of authority, the proposal calls upon the Security Council to take any measures necessary to ensure the U.N.'s control.

[35] *Monthly Chronicle* (Dec., 1966), 66.
[36] *Monthly Chronicle* (Nov., 1966), 20-26.

The least forceful of the suggestions was submitted by Canada, Italy, and the United States. It calls for the creation of a council which will make a comprehensive survey of the situation in South West Africa and recommend to the twenty-second regular session of the General Assembly ways in which it can effectively aid the independence of South West Africa. The committee members from Czechoslovakia and Russia charged that this proposal was a colonialist scheme designed to perpetuate South Africa's domination of South West Africa.

A compromise suggestion sponsored by Chile and Mexico provides for the creation of a council which eventually will assume full responsibility for the administration of South West Africa, but which immediately will assist the South West Africans in establishing a legislative assembly and a politically responsible government. The proposal does not provide for the use of force, but recommends negotiations between the council and South Africa in accordance with the terms of Resolution 2145 which terminated the mandate.[37]

The fact that the fourteen-member *ad hoc* committee could not agree on a proposed solution is indicative of a widening gulf among assembly members on the South West Africa case. While the Soviet Union had always given the impression that it would support the use of force in this instance, and while it still backs the proposal of Ethiopia, Nigeria, Senegal, and the United Arab Republic, it now indicates that the use of force would exceed the terms of the charter. The United States' attitude is indicated by its sponsorship of a weak and essentially meaningless proposal.

Current attitudes in the General Assembly point toward speedy passage of a resolution declaring the independence of South West Africa under United Nations' supervision. Passing such a resolution may pose little difficulty, but enforcement is another matter. At present, force is on the side of the White South African, not the native or the United Nations. If the United Nations sends a police force into the territory, which seems unlikely, a war involving

[37] *Monthly Chronicle* (April, 1967), 11-16.

South Africa and possibly Southern Rhodesia and Portugal might result. If such a force is not deployed, the United Nations would be left only with economic sanctions, which historically have been a weak device. As in the Southern Rhodesia case, the United Kingdom and the United States would be the two powers most extensively involved. Without the full backing of these two nations, South Africa's economy scarcely could be damaged. More than one-third of South Africa's trade is with the United States and the United Kingdom. Britain's investment in South Africa totals about one billion pounds sterling, while United States' holdings are near $500,000,000 and are increasing.[38] South Africa's economy is based primarily on coal. Oil represents only 10 percent of fuel requirements, and even if an oil embargo were complete, it seems likely that at least a year would elapse before its effects would be felt seriously.[39]

Because of Britain's domestic economic problems and because of her desire to effect the downfall of the South Rhodesian government, Britain's position on the South West Africa issue is unclear. At the request of Britain, the Security Council on December 16, 1966, adopted a resolution calling for selective mandatory sanctions against Southern Rhodesia on such commodities as asbestos, iron ore, chrome, pig iron, sugar, tobacco, copper, meat, hides, and skins. All nations were asked to prevent their nationals and vessels from supplying oil, arms, and military equipment to Southern Rhodesia. The delegate from the United Kingdom stated that although economic sanctions instituted by his and other governments had not borne out earlier forecasts, the Rhodesian economy had been dented significantly. Exports had been cut by about 40 percent from £143 million in 1965 to a current annual rate of £80 million.[40]

Because the Rhodesian embargo cannot be effective as long as supplies bound for Rhodesia move freely through South Africa,

[38] Gross, *Foreign Affairs* (Oct., 1966), 41.
[39] Philip Mason, "South Africa and the World: Some Maxims and Axioms," *Foreign Affairs* (Oct., 1964), 155.
[40] *Monthly Chronicle* (Jan., 1967), 6-8.

Britain might be tempted to agree to economic sanctions against South Africa. Most observers agree that an economic embargo is not likely to be effective unless accompanied by a blockade. If this were used, the naval power of the United States would become a key factor. Because of the military involvement in Vietnam, however, the United States undoubtedly will urge moderation.

These issues involving racial discrimination and colonialism are proving to be a tough test case for the effectiveness and power of the United Nations, and, in the eyes of some nations, will either establish the U.N. as a firm power or doom it to ineffectiveness. Because of the failure of the International Court to rule in the South West Africa case, many nations—particularly the small African nations—have dismissed the court as a meaningful body in international relations.

While the majority of nations feel that the South African government cannot resist forever the mounting tide of criticism, the South Africans feel that the newly independent African states run by natives will become economically and politically bankrupt, and the world then will realize how wronged South Africa has been. Increasingly, the South Africans are attempting to promote themselves as a flourishing capitalistic system besieged by world Communism and betrayed by most of the other capitalistic states.

The efforts of the United Nations have had some effect on South African policy, and South African officials now are concerned with outside appearances and world opinion. The South African government has drawn up a plan by which the natives of South West Africa supposedly would control a greater share of the government and the economic wealth of that territory. This proposed five-year development plan grew from suggestions made by a committee appointed by the South African government. This Odendaal Committee concluded that the solution to South West Africa's problems would be integration of the territory into the Republic of South Africa with the provision of a greater share of the territory's wealth and benefits for the natives.[41] The mem-

[41] "U.N. Report on Mining Companies," *Africa Digest*, XII (Feb., 1965), 109-10.

bers of the United Nations have not been deceived by this change in South Africa's policy, because the provisions of the plan do not provide for changes which will really benefit the natives.

The development plan would establish hydroelectric power projects, increase the water supply, construct main roads, build local roads for the nonwhite areas, construct a new airport, increase health and hospital facilities, and build additional schools.[42] It is not clear, however, that the benefits of this plan will not be channeled toward the Europeans of South West Africa rather than toward its native population.

The plan also provides for "accelerated progress towards self-government for the various groups in South West Africa along the same lines as in the Republic." Each African group would have a legislative council headed by an executive committee. The Bushmen were not included among these groups, because they have not yet advanced far enough to merit any form of self-government.[43] Development along the same lines as in the Republic of South Africa means continuation of apartheid with the natives having no voice in important matters. The native councils, which the Republic government has offered to establish, theoretically have existed since 1925. The five-year plan is significant in one respect only, in revealing that South African officials are worried about the future course of events, but not worried enough to make genuine reforms. In fact, latest policy statements indicate that South Africa will resist United Nations actions with force, if necessary.

[42] "South West Africa," *Africa Annual* (1965), 120.
[43] "South West Africa," *Africa Annual* (1965), 119.

EIGHT:

AN EVALUATION

Although the United Nations has not yet found an acceptable solution to the South West Africa problem, it has made at least seven noteworthy accomplishments in the case. Perhaps the greatest accomplishment is the most obvious. By discussing South Africa's conduct toward its mandate, the U.N. has kept that issue alive and has provided the medium through which the collective protest and the organized effort of many nations have been channeled. Through the United Nations, South Africa and the world have been aware of the strong feelings of the African, Asian, and Communist countries on the South West Africa question. These strong emotions have been restrained somewhat, however, by the attitudes of the remaining members, who believed that every effort to negotiate the dispute peacefully should be made. Because of this restraining action, only after it was clear that all else had failed was a more forceful policy adopted. Even so, collectively, the nations have accomplished more than they could have individually.

The United Nations, in conjunction with the International Court of Justice, has defined the status of South West Africa. When the League of Nations ceased to exist, it was not clear where sovereignty over South West Africa resided. The International Court concluded that the territory possessed an international status and that the United Nations was the heir to the rights and obligations of the League.

As a consequence of the General Assembly's refusal to approve the area's incorporation into the Union, and as a result of the court's opinion that the territory possessed an international status, the United Nations has prevented the complete annexation of South West Africa by South Africa. In 1949, South Africa virtually annexed the mandate, but there has been no international recognition of that action. Not even the government of South Africa dares ignore that fact, and undoubtedly their actions have been restrained by the United Nations' objections on this point. The court's decision that South West Africa was an international territory removed all legal justification for annexation.

Through the efforts of the General Assembly and the International Court of Justice, a system of international supervision over the administration of the mandate has been provided. While this supervision has failed in many respects, it has had some beneficial results. Even without the cooperation of the South African government, various committees of the United Nations have succeeded in making available a vast amount of information about conditions within the mandate. This information has confirmed the belief of the majority of U.N. members that South Africa is unfit to rule South West Africa. While it cannot be proven, it is possible that South African actions have been tempered by this supervisory effort.

There is no doubt that the United Nations has contributed to the increased isolation of the Republic of South Africa. Perhaps no other nation is so despised and so alone. Intensified contempt and increased isolation can be regarded as desirable developments, however, only if they bring positive results. The South Africans have not abandoned apartheid, but they are maintaining the policy at a tremendous cost. Perhaps some day they will conclude that the cost is too dear.

Finally, the United Nations has to an undetermined degree affected opinions and actions within both the Republic of South Africa and South West Africa. Today, as never before, the basic tenets of South Africa's policies in South West Africa are being challenged. This challenge emanates from three separate but related sources—United Nations' actions, measures taken by some nations acting independently of the United Nations,[1] and

[1] For example, thirty independent African nations agreed to work toward the elimination of colonialism and white domination in Africa, and Ghana established an economic boycott against South Africa.

the course of events within South West Africa itself. The combined weight of these three forces is causing some South African
nationals, who view South African policy in the light of world
criticism, to question the correctness of South Africa's policy.
These critics are still a small minority, but they are growing.

One of the most outspoken leaders of this group is J. D.
Du P. Basson, one of South West Africa's representatives in the
Union Parliament. Basson and his followers charge that South
Africa recently has suffered five major shocks, all making the
nation more insecure, because of its policies. The first of these
blows is the institution of contentious proceedings before the
International Court of Justice. The second is the loss of Commonwealth membership as the result of pressure from Black Africa.[2]
The third is the increasing sharpness of United Nations resolutions
and actions against South Africa. A fourth blow is the increasing
political activity among natives of South West Africa and of
Portuguese Angola, which poses a threat to South Africa. If
the Portuguese cannot maintain their hold over the natives in
Angola, this would encourage the natives in South West Africa
to rebel. Basson felt that the greatest blow of all to South Africa
is the collapse of that country's international prestige. Because
South Africa and South West Africa have divided populations,
they cannot afford to be isolated.[3]

Basson's fears were shared by the leader of the opposition party,
Sir De Villiers Graaff. He said that if the South Africans did
not find realistic and practical solutions to their own race problems,
they might find solutions imposed upon them from outside.[4]

Though internal criticism is growing, it is doubtful that the
South African government will alter its course before the United
Nations is forced to apply sanctions. While the efforts of the

[2] There appear to have been two primary motives behind this withdrawal.
South Africa was not willing to modify its racial policies to meet Commonwealth demands, and the Afrikaner population wanted to break all ties with
the British.

[3] Union of South Africa, House of Assembly Debates, April 17, 1961, cols.
4768-69.

[4] South Africa House of Assembly Debates, April 10, 1961, cols. 4153-60.

United Nations have had a restraining effect on the government, the organization has been unsuccessful in forcing the South Africans to place the mandate under trusteeship or to abandon the application of apartheid within the territory. However, if the United Nations had not interceded, it is likely that the natives of South West Africa would have been subjected to treatment which was even more inhumane, and it is almost certain that South Africa would have annexed the territory.

While the natives of South West Africa are still existing under the policy of apartheid, they are aware that they are no longer alone in their struggle against the South African government. U.N. efforts have made them more hopeful. However, the natives cannot free themselves at present, because they lack sufficint organization, education, political sophistication, and wealth. The policy of apartheid has succeeded in keeping political power away from the natives, so the immediate fate of the natives of South West Africa rests with the members of the United Nations.

Even though the United Nations has made a number of accomplishments in the South West Africa case, it has failed to achieve totally any of its four major goals. One of the primary objectives of the United Nations was to secure a trusteeship agreement from the South African government for South West Africa. Since the International Court of Justice advised that South Africa was not legally obligated to accept this solution, the United Nations was left powerless on this point.

After this defeat the chief objective of the United Nations was to secure a settlement which would guarantee United Nations' supervision of the administration of South West Africa. This has not been successful because the organization has not applied sufficient force. The South Africans are aware of the consequences which would result from this supervision, and they will not submit on this point as long as there remains any alternative. Their alternative has been to ignore the opinions of the International Court, the United Nations, and the world.

Since the United Nations could not accomplish either of these goals, it has sought to supervise South African administration without the cooperation of that government. This supervisory effort has met with only partial success. The United Nations does not have access to all the necessary information, and it cannot send observers to South West Africa, because South African authorities have the legal right to deny their admission. The United Nations has the potential power for forcing a solution to the dispute, but it cannot force cooperation.

A fourth major goal of the United Nations was to force the South African government to abandon apartheid in South West Africa. The United Nations has made the South West African natives aware that they are treated unjustly, but it has not been able to remove existing racial barriers. The natives still work, study, travel, and live according to the dictates of apartheid. The South African government legally exercises much control over South West Africa, because the mandate was ruled as an integral part of the mandatory, and the agreement stated that South Africa's laws could be applied within the territory. The United Nations cannot order committees and agencies into such an area to abolish apartheid unless the South African government is willing to permit such actions.

Many foes of apartheid and colonialism believed that the International Court of Justice would provide the United Nations with the legal justification for ending South African domination over South West Africa by concluding that South Africa had violated its "sacred trust" in South West Africa and that the mandatory no longer was entitled to rule. The United Nations would then be armed legally to take whatever measures seemed practical and desirable. While it is improbable that South Africa would have abandoned its policies peaceably, the court's verdict can serve only to strengthen South Africa's resistance to reform. However, the court possibly was correct to refuse the case. While the South West Africa issue is not without a legal solution, it will not be settled on the basis of legalisms. The motivating factors in the dispute are political and racial, and the case eventually must be settled on these grounds.

Short of a total reversal in the trend of world affairs, what ultimately will transpire in South West Africa is predictable. Eventually, South African exploitation of the territory will end. Ultimately, apartheid will fall. The process may be long and costly, but colonialism and white supremacy are dying. Whether the United Nations can be a guiding force for peaceful change in South West Africa remains to be seen.

APPENDIX

South West African Mandate Agreement

The Council of the League of Nations:

Whereas by Article 119 of the Treaty of Peace with Germany signed at Versailles on June 28th, 1919, Germany renounced in favour of the Principal Allied and Associated Powers all her rights over her overseas possessions, including therein German South-West Africa; and

Whereas the Principal Allied and Associated Powers agreed that, in accordance with Article 22, Part I (Covenant of the League of Nations) of the said Treaty, a Mandate should be conferred upon His Britannic Majesty to be exercised on his behalf by the Government of the Union of South Africa to administer the territory aforementioned, and have proposed that the Mandate should be formulated in the following terms; and

Whereas His Britannic Majesty, for and on behalf of the Government of the Union of South Africa, has agreed to accept the Mandate in respect to the said territory and has undertaken to exercise it on behalf of the League of Nations in accordance with the following provisions; and

Whereas, by the aforementioned Article 22, paragraph 8, it is provided that the degree of authority, control or administration to be exercised by the Mandatory of the League, shall be explicitly defined by the Council of the League of Nations:

Confirming the said Mandate, defines its terms as follows;

Article 1. The territory over which a Mandate is conferred upon His Britannic Majesty for and on behalf of the Government of the Union of South Africa (hereinafter called the Mandatory) comprises the territory which formerly constituted the German Protectorate of South-West Africa.

Article 2. The Mandatory shall have full power of administration and legislation over the territory subject to the present Mandate as an integral portion of the Union of South Africa, and may apply the laws of the Union of South Africa to the territory, subject to such local modifications as circumstances may require.

The Mandatory shall promote to the utmost the material and moral well-being and the social progress of the inhabitants of the territory subject to the present Mandate.

Article 3. The Mandatory shall see that the slave trade is prohibited, and that no forced labour is permitted, except for essential public works and services, and then only for adequate remuneration.

The Mandatory shall also see that the traffic in arms and ammunition is controlled in accordance with principles analogous to those laid down in the Covenant relating to the control of the arms traffic, signed on September 10th, 1919, or in any covention amending the same.

The supply of intoxicating spirits and beverages to the natives shall be prohibited.

Article 4. The military training of the natives, otherwise than for purposes of internal police and the local defense of the territory, shall be prohibited. Furthermore, no military or naval bases shall be established in the territory.

Article 5. Subject to the provisions of any local law for the maintenance of public order and public morals, the Mandatory shall ensure in the territory freedom of conscience and the free exercise of all forms of worship, and shall allow all missionaries, nationals of any State Member of the League of Nations, to enter into, travel and reside in the territory for the purpose of prosecuting their calling.

Article 6. The Mandatory shall make the Council of the League of Nations an annual report to the satisfaction of the Council, containing full information with regard to the territory, and indicating the measures taken to carry out the obligation assumed under Articles 2, 3, 4, and 5.

Article 7. The consent of the Council of the League of Nations is required for any modification of the terms of the present Mandate.

The Mandatory agrees that, if any dispute whatever should arise between the Mandatory and another Member of the League of Nations relating to the interpretation or the application of the provisions of the Mandate, such dispute, if it cannot be settled by negotiation, shall be submitted to the Permanent Court of International Justice provided for by Article 14 of the Covenant of the League of Nations.

The present Declaration shall be deposited in the Archives of the League of Nations. Certified copies shall be forwarded by the Secretary-General of the League of Nations to all Powers Signatories of the Treaty of Peace with Germany.[1]

[1] *International Legislation,* ed. Manley O. Hudson, 9 vols. (Washington, Carnegie Endowment For International Peace, 1931), I, 57-60.

INDEX